2012: Political Self-Righteousness,

A Time for Self-Reflection

Frank Coyle

DEDICATION

To my wife of thirty-three years, Joanne: Thank you for
your patience, your understanding, your support, and most
importantly for letting me build my life with you. You have
made family the most important thing in our life. Now that
we have become grandparents together, it is wonderful to
share our love with a new generation. Also, thanks for just
being fun. To my two grown children, Christopher and
Kelly, and my son-in-law, Adrian: thank you for the joy you
have brought to my life.

May 4, 2012

CONTENTS

1. INTRODUCTION

"Election 2012" is the most divisive campaign season that America has ever seen. And, this is not good for America.

Over one billion dollars will be spent this year on the presidential election campaign. Large staffs of organizers, political strategists, pollsters, and phone callers will be employed. Countless hours of radio and television commercials will help stimulate the economy. But what will it tell us about ourselves, where our country is heading, or how we should get there?

It was not until the end of April that the Republicans anointed Governor Romney as their presumed candidate. However, the republican debates, the banter between the candidates and both parties' spin machines have already framed the 2012 presidential election campaign: class warfare, health care, the national debt and jobs, jobs, jobs. Or more simply: it's the economy stupid!

Most Americans know the issues facing our nation. Most Americans have ideas of what should be done. What Americans are looking for is a way to get things done.

The economy is the biggest issue for most Americans. The Democrats are proposing to raise taxes on the wealthy, and redistribute the wealth to the less fortunate who will spend the money rather than save (or invest) it. The Republicans are proposing to cut taxes so that businesses will realize more profits and use the profits to hire more people. The democrats also propose more regulation to preclude future economic chaos caused by unscrupulous businesses. The republicans are calling for less regulation to make business more productive.

This is an over simplification, but the message most Americans are hearing is: class warfare versus trickle down and more versus less regulation. It is big government versus small government. This is NOT what this campaign SHOULD be about. Neither camp is talking about what this campaign should be about. Maybe they do not get it - or maybe they do not believe enough in themselves to take it on. In fact, the billion dollars that will be spent this campaign season will only make the real problem facing America worse.

We are in a death spiral of political gridlock. Washington is not able to practice the art of politics (which is compromise) because of ideological _self-righteousness_. It was a sad day when the moderator asked for a show of hands from all the republican candidates who would be willing to raise taxes by one dollar for every ten dollars of spending cuts – not a single hand went up.

The Republicans have made the mistake of labeling their ideological self-righteous members – the Tea Party. The Tea Party began with (and retains) a no-compromise position on raising taxes. It is because of the Tea Party that the Republican candidates could not raise their hands to offer $1 of taxes for $10 of spending cuts. More recently, the Tea Party has established a no-compromise position on a slew of social issues.

The Democrats have not labeled their ideologues (smart move), but they do exist. The Democrats self-righteous members have a no-compromise position on spending cuts to entitlement programs. The Democrats have even run a television commercial that depicts Congressman Ryan of Wisconsin throwing grandma (in a wheel-chair) over a cliff. The commercial was *critical* of Congressman Ryan's proposed budget bill that included cuts to some of our entitlement programs.

If we abide by both the Republican's and Democrat's extreme ideologies, we cannot raise taxes and we cannot cut spending. Has anybody noticed that the national debt is scheduled to increase *FOREVER*?

Politics in America have never been as polarized as they are today. Talk radio, ideological television shows, and the twenty-four by seven news cycle have heightened all Americans' awareness of who is on which side. We are instantly alerted when somebody from either the Red (Republican) team or the Blue (Democrat) team state an opinion (or even a thought) that is not in accordance with the team's designated talking points. That poor individual is no longer a valued member of their affiliated party. The media has turned politics into sport. Just as we Americans are loyal to our favorite sports team, we are loyal to our favorite political team (or party). Everything is black or white. No gray is permitted on this playing field. You are either all in, or you are all out. It must be good for ratings or the media would not continue to play it up. But it is not good for America.

Americans have always been passionate. America has always had bickering. We also had statesmen who could find the common ground, find a reasoned solution and communicate to both their party members and non-party members the merits of moving forward in a spirit of compromise. Have you seen any of that lately?

America has always been at its best when faced with its largest challenges: the Great Depression, World Wars I and II, and most recently, the Great Recession. Remember when Congress was so scared by Treasury Secretary Paulson that they actually rushed a bi-partisan bill to inject billions of dollars into the collapsing financial system? That bill prevented a systemic failure that would have surely resulted in the Great Depression II. Remember when a bi-partisan congress passed a $787 billion stimulus plan to jump start the economy? This happened after the banking crisis was addressed (if not yet cured) and businesses were like deer in headlights - scared to death of the uncertainty that prevailed at the time. Businesses hoarded their cash, slashed jobs, and prepared for economic Armageddon? Most Americans believed that economic Armageddon was at our door step.

It was not that long ago that, when faced with a real crisis, Congress was able to act (the banking system bailout and the stimulus package). It appears that the only time Congress can act is when an inevitable catastrophe provides them with a cloak of protection. However, the inevitable catastrophe must be very near term. The catastrophe must be scheduled to hit America before the next election. If not, it will just have to wait. Election campaigns are clearly more important than matters related to the demise of the American economy.

The spin machines are stating that this election is the most important in history. They claim that it will determine the direction of our nation _forever_ – big or small government. This election will _NOT_ determine the course of our nation forever. This election will most likely leave us _directionless_. It would be better if we picked a direction. Then we would have a basis upon which to correct our course. Unfortunately, this election will result in even more political gridlock than we have today. Therefore, we will continue to be adrift at sea - with no leadership at the helm.

Contrary to the spin machines rhetoric, this election is not the most important in history – but it is important. This election is important because it comes at a point in time where America has to learn how to function in the new twenty-four by seven news cycle, social media, blogospheres, and the "it is my way or the highway" world that has been created in the past decade (or two). It is important because we need to elect leaders that can lead us to this new way of functioning.

This election is also important because this campaign season will spew a vast quantity of negativity upon we Americans. All this negativity should make us pause, and hit the reset button. We must realize that we have allowed ourselves to be manipulated by the spin machines into becoming irrational human beings. It is time for we Americans to reclaim civility in our politics. It is time to admit that "the other side" may actually have some valid points.

The negativity that this election campaign will put forth will cause some Americans to despise the "other side's" candidate. Worse yet; it will cause some Americans to despise other civilians that support the other side. After the elections are over, an atmosphere of mistrust among our elected leaders and civilians alike will preclude any compromise on the challenges that America faces - the same atmosphere that already exists today – but worse.

America faces very real challenges. Unfortunately, these challenges are long-term challenges. The type that if not addressed today will become catastrophes tomorrow. Tomorrow's catastrophe will cause real fear, even panic. That fear will inspire action. Unfortunately, it will be too late. The challenges we face will result in a crisis that cannot be fixed with a point-in-time, panic piece of legislation (like the banking system bailout or stimulus package). We will be facing the situation that Greece is currently facing - one that has no quick fix – one that will result in enormous human hardship.

Politics as usual will result in America continuing down the path to Greece. But, there is another way forward!

2. THE ISSUES

The issues that have (so far this campaign season) been kicked around as the matters that concern America's future will be listed and defined. Following the definition, different positions on the issue will be presented. These issues, definitions and positions are from the author's perspective. The author is the guy "From the Middle". The positions from the "Far Left" and the "Far Right" are also from the author's perspective. These are the positions that the "Guy from the Middle" is hearing from the spin machines.

Most Americans are moderate in their political views. It is the media that creates the illusion that half of us are Far Left and the other half Far Right. The media even has many of us believing that we are either Far Right or Far Left. It's no fun if you don't have a team to route for – or an enemy to attack.

If the author is not the guy "From the Middle" – he is the guy in the middle that leans a little right. Most importantly, he is a little guy. It is time for the little guy to have a say in this campaign mess.

Topics as diverse as colonies on the moon, Iran's nuclear capabilities, contraception and religious freedom have been covered. Republicans have been born with silver spoons in their mouths, and the democrats are all the anti-Christ. Ann Romney never worked a day in her life and Michelle Obama flies off in Air Force One to vacation in the South of Spain. America practices hardball politics. No wonder Americans make policy making so personal – the media makes it personal. And, there is a dearth of leaders to shine the light of the American ideals.

As Winston Churchill once said, "Democracy is the worst form of government on earth - except for every other form of government."

The long list of issues and positions demonstrates how diverse we are as thinkers – _NOT_ how divided we are as a people. The large number of issues being debated makes it hard to see the forest for the trees. However, when you are spending a billion dollars, you have to carpet bomb the electorate. One issue that may seem trivial to most may be the deciding factor for some. This list was developed in April of 2012, so it will necessarily be missing the late campaign season "gotchas". The list is in no particular order:

1. Jobs, jobs, jobs

Definition: Unemployment is still above 8% but has been steadily declining. Most Americans know someone that is out of work. In some months, the decline in unemployment was not due to more jobs - but rather due to the large number of Americans that have given up hope of finding a job.

Far Left: Jobs can be created by government spending. Once the government has created the jobs, the stimulated economy will begin to grow on its own and allow the government to back off of its stimulus spending.

Far Right: Jobs can only be created by private business. The government will only create a short term recovery that will end as soon as the stimulus dollars are stopped.

From the Middle: The economy contraction of 2008 required massive government intervention to prevent an even worse economic situation. Now that a recovery is under way, we need to focus on our debt problem. We also need some creative changes to convert the corporate recovery into jobs for the American people. The sluggishness of our recovery will most likely result in some months where unemployment ticks up a bit. If this happens, we should not allow the psychology of the market to spook ourselves into the feared "double dip" recession. We face a rocky road to full-recovery. We should expect some ups and downs on the jobs count. The recovery is sluggish and there are a lot of people that have left the jobs market - who will one day return. Overall, our direction is (and should continue to be) positive. The truth of the matter is that 8% unemployment may be the new norm. The "Fixing the Economy" chapter discusses what we should do to fix that problem.

2. Manufacturing jobs

Definition: Jobs in manufacturing facilities generally pay higher wages than those in the service industry. The problem is that the United States has been losing much of its manufacturing base to foreign countries (i.e.: China and Mexico) due to the low cost of labor in those countries. The issue here is not the jobs themselves. The issue is - how do we make the United States more competitive in the global economy? If we do not become more competitive, we will continue to purchase more goods from foreign countries while selling less of our products back to them. That means our wealth will be slowly drained out of America and into the hands of our foreign competitors. Our wealth has been draining for over thirty years due to our negative balance of trade. We have not had a surplus in our balance of trade since 1975. This is one of the two major factors that have made America a debtor nation. The other factor is our government spending more than it collects in taxes – but that is for other issues to discuss.

Far Left: Tax breaks for manufacturing businesses.

Far Right: Tax breaks for *ALL* businesses.

From the Middle: Stop taxing businesses and only tax people. When people buy the manufactured products they are paying the business taxes embedded in the purchase price of the product. When we tax the businesses, the people of foreign countries are paying the embedded taxes on our exports – which make us less competitive. We also need to become more energy self-sufficient so that American businesses have the advantage of inexpensive energy (as compared to the rest of the world). Finally, we need to replace the Affordable Care Act with a single-payer, socialized health care system that *reduces* the cost of health care. The Affordable Care Act has increased the cost of health care and has, therefore, made us less globally competitive. That is it: three items that will make us more competitive in the global economy; 1) inexpensive energy, 2) lower health care costs, and 3) less business taxes. Implementing these three items will reduce the cost of production so that we can sell our products at a lower price in the global marketplace. Thus, our economy will grow, we will balance our trade, expand our tax base of working people, and help (a little) solve the other big issue we are facing – our government spending more than it collects in taxes. Tax collection will rise, but we will still need to implement some spending cuts. The "Fixing the Economy" expands upon this discussion and also includes thoughts on how we can compete with the $2 per hour labor that is available in China, Mexico and other parts of the world.

3. Unemployment Benefits

<u>Definition</u>: Should we continue paying benefits for 99 weeks? If so, what should the recipients do to *earn* this benefit?

<u>Far Left</u>: Unemployment benefits should be paid forever. The people getting those benefits are out of work due to no fault of their own.

<u>Far Right</u>: Cut unemployment benefits after a few months because getting paid to do nothing just provides people with the incentive to stay home and enjoy their government-paid vacation. Furthermore, people collecting unemployment should have to do something to get their benefits (i.e.: community work, job training)

<u>From the Middle</u>: Economic times are tough. Extended benefits are needed, but six months is probably the appropriate term. Helping the unemployed get work through job training is a good idea. Maybe we need a shorter work week. The automation of work has reduced the amount of people needed in the workplace. The post office is a perfect example of this. More on this will be discussed in "Fixing the Economy" chapter. As an aside, businesses pay the majority of unemployment benefits through taxes. Therefore, those "government-paid vacations" are not really paid for by the government.

4. Bailout of the Banks

Definition: The banks created their own crisis of liquidity through bad lending practices and cock-eyed derivative trading. After creating this liquidity problem, Congress bailed them out. Congress passed a bill to provide billions of dollars to the banks so that there would not be a "systematic failure" of the banking system. Systematic failure is when one bank fails and cannot pay other banks to whom it owes money. The other banks do not get paid by the first bank and then they fail.   A chain reaction of bank failures then occurs. The result of this chain reaction is that there are no banks left to lend money. Maybe we did have that systematic failure. Although there was a bank on every street in America, there were none willing to lend any money.

Far Left: This was a major accomplishment. It prevented the Great Recession II – there were no other alternatives. Allowing the system to fail would have brought great harm to all Americans and even caused a global depression.

Far Right: Let them fail. We all learned the new term "moral hazard". If you screw up, you pay the price. We should never bailout anyone ever again. The government just slows down the inevitable process of "creative destruction" that the marketplace will perform.

From the Middle: Whew, dodged a bullet that time. Why did Secretary Paulson allow Lehman Brothers to fail? That really spooked the financial system. Did Secretary Paulson's past life at Goldman Sachs (the archrival of Lehman Brothers) have anything to do with that decision? Why haven't any of the bankers been locked up yet? The bankers that created this disaster are crooks that perpetrated acts that have cost the American taxpayers billions – no, trillions of dollars. We want some of that "moral hazard" for the bankers!

5. Dodd-Frank

Definition: A new law (cosponsored by Senator Chris Dodd of Connecticut and Congressman Barney Frank of Massachusetts) was passed that puts into place a new government regulator that will oversee the financial industry. The law was a direct result of the bank bailouts. It is intended to prevent the government from ever having to bailout the financial system again. It also includes measures to protect consumers from unscrupulous financial companies (like banks and brokerages). The law even gives the new regulators the authority to require a large financial institution to divest some of its holdings if it is deemed to have become "too big to fail". The new regulator appears to have unlimited authority and an unlimited budget. The new regulator is a part of the Federal Reserve Bank – so it has a lot of autonomy. The law is so vague that businesses are worried that it may intrude on non-financial businesses. For example; will the regulator oversee a business that charges interest on late payments? If we look at the big banks that were bailed out – do they NOT all remain too big to fail? What will this new regulator do about that?

Far Left: This is a great accomplishment.

Far Right: This is overkill. We already have enough laws to regulate the financial industry. This is causing a lot of uncertainty in the business community. The uncertainty is bad for the economy.

From the Middle: We are with the Far Right on this one. Furthermore, does anyone ever remove the old laws when

new ones are created? We have way too much regulation.
Please enforce the old laws and lock up a few of those
unscrupulous bankers that caused us all so much pain and
suffering. New laws will place more reporting requirements
on the financial companies. Thus, they will make those
companies less productive. The new laws will not,
however, scare any of the unscrupulous bankers from
repeating the mistakes of the past. Until we use the laws
already on the books, unscrupulous people will find ways to
cheat the system. _Enforcement_ of laws make people
behave as they should. The mere existence of unenforced
laws does not provide a deterrent against anything. Since
we have _NOT_ enforced any of our existing laws – it is just a
matter of time until we see the repeat of the cock-eyed
derivative trading that caused the 2008 banking collapse
(or some other financial shenanigans). Financial
shenanigans are prone to happen after long periods of
monetary easing (low interest rates). When money is
cheap, people (aka: bankers) look for ways to exploit the
cheap money. When money is cheap _and_ there is no law
enforcement in town – you really have a recipe for disaster.
Guess where we are right now?

6. Bailout of the Car Companies

Definition: GM and Chrysler were given federal loans to
keep them afloat during the Great Recession. These loans
were out of the taxpayers coffers.

Far Left: This was a great accomplishment. The federal
loans provided time to the car companies that allowed
them to stay in business and maintain good manufacturing
jobs. Furthermore, the car companies are now profitable
again and paying back all the money the government lent
them.

Far Right: Let them fail. The only reason that they are profitable now is because even with the government loans, they did, in fact, fail. They filed for bankruptcy and renegotiated their union contracts.

From the Middle: It does seem as though the government is picking winners and losers. Big businesses were bailed out while small businesses struggled without any support. However, the big companies' success does have a trickle down impact on the overall economy. So if you have to pick a winner, this was a good pick. It was great to see unions realize the reality of the global economy and renegotiate their contracts. This is a trend that all unions must follow so that America can compete in the global economy.

7. Taxes

Definition: The government has to either raise more revenue (taxes) or cut spending in order to bring our fiscal house to order. This issue will deal with the tax side of the equation. Specific issues like Social Security, Medicare, Military, and the Affordable Care Act will deal with the spending side.

Far Left: The rich do not pay enough taxes. Warren Buffet's secretary pays more in taxes than he does. The Occupy Wall Street movement shines a light on the inequities in America. The top 1% is costing the remaining 99% too much.

Far Right: The rich pay too much. If they were taxed less, they would have more money to hire more people. The economy would grow. The larger economy would provide a larger tax base and thus more government revenue. Furthermore, 50% of Americans pay no federal income tax and almost 50% of Americans receive some form of federal aid.

From the Middle: We must raise _income_ taxes on everybody (people _NOT_ businesses) and cut spending. It is wrong for half of Americans to _NOT_ pay any federal income tax. Allow the Bush tax cuts to expire in stages over the next few years - for over $500K earners at the end of this year, for over $200K earners at the end of 2013, and for _ALL_ Americans at the end of 2014. The capital gains tax of 15% should _NOT_ be changed. Capital gains and dividends are earned on money that people have saved and invested. When they earned that money (before they could invest it), it was taxed at the full _income tax_ rate. To continually tax capital gains and dividends at the income tax rate is unfair. Most of our elderly population live off of their social security and the capital gains and dividends of their investments. To subject our elderly population to higher taxes is not fair. They have worked too hard all their life. We cannot make their retirement less fulfilling than they had worked to achieve. Also, the lower tax rate on capital gains is an incentive for investment in American businesses. The need for incentives to invest in American manufacturing will be discussed in the "Fixing the Economy" chapter of this book. As for our entitlement programs - why are 48.6% of Americans receiving federal aid? We have to re-evaluate our social safety-net.

8. End the Fed

Definition: Eliminate the country's central bank - the Federal Reserve Bank. The Federal Reserve Bank makes monetary policy decisions without any oversight from Congress. To help alleviate the Great Recession, the Federal Reserve Bank lowered interest rates to near zero (for inter-bank lending) and purchased billions of dollars worth of the "toxic assets" (mortgage backed securities) that the banks created. The Fed called these purchases "monetary easing".

Far Left: Absurd. This is the foundation of our financial system and has served America well in managing our monetary policy for years. Furthermore, its autonomy allows it to take necessary action swiftly. Once the Fed lowered interest rates to zero everyone thought they were out of bullets to help remedy the ailing economy. The monetary easing was a stroke of genius that showed everybody that the Fed is creative and very helpful. Let the Fed stay autonomous to stay effective.

Far Right: Dismantle the Federal Reserve System. It is no longer needed. Banks can lend each other money. The marketplace will adjust interest rates to match the prevailing supply and demand conditions of any point in time. There is no oversight of the Fed's activities and that is a recipe for danger.

From the Middle: The middle is with the Far Left on this one. Which of those big banks would have purchased those toxic assets? What ever became of those toxic assets? Are we taxpayers going to pay for them when their toxicity is accounted for by the bookkeepers? Has it been mentioned that the bankers that caused this mess should be locked up?

9. Social Security

Definition: Should we means test Social Security benefits, should we raise the retirement age, and should we privatize Social Security? This is one of our largest entitlement programs. It provides the basic level of support to our elderly population.

<u>Far Left</u>: No changes are needed to social security. To means test the benefit would diminish the dignity of those who still receive the benefit. Americans have paid into this system their entire working life and they were promised this benefit.

<u>Far Right</u>: Means test the benefits, raise the retirement age, and privatize the system. We are going broke and we have tough choices to make. This is low hanging fruit.

<u>From the Middle</u>:   Raise the retirement age in stages until it reaches seventy-two for everybody (it is currently sixty-seven for anyone younger than fifty-two). Means test the benefit but establish a moderately high cutoff point for not receiving the benefit (e.g.: $100K). That way it will save us some money but retain the dignity of receiving the benefit. Consider privatization for younger workers. As an aside, when Social Security became law in 1930, the retirement age was set at sixty-five. However, the life-expectancy at that time was fifty-eight for men and sixty-two for women. The law was not designed for a life-expectancy of eighty years.

10. Medicare

<u>Definition</u>: Very similar to the Social Security discussion – but Medicare is our fastest growing expense. Should we plan on the $500 billion cuts that are embedded in the Affordable Care Act?

<u>Far Left</u>: The Affordable Care Act will take care of the nation's health care. Eventually, the problems with the Affordable Care Act will be corrected and the country will have a true, single-payer, socialized health care system. Then, everyone will be on the Affordable Care Act's health care plan.

Far Right: Save Medicare. We cannot alienate the senior voting block (they actually vote on a consistent basis). We promised our seniors this benefit. We should not cut the $500 billion that the Affordable Care Act includes. Instead, we should repeal the Affordable Care Act and focus all our medical spending on the retired population. Those with jobs can purchase their own health care. We will allow more competition in the marketplace, so it will be more affordable. Those without jobs can get charitable help or just visit the emergency room.

From the Middle: Let's just get on with the rest of the civilized world and follow the Far Left's ultimate goal of a single-payer, socialized health care system. Those that can afford premium health care will be able to purchase "add-on coverage" much the same way Medicare advantage plans work today. We already have socialized health care in America. We just deny its existence. Laws that require emergency rooms to accept any patient regardless of whether or not they have health care insurance is socialized health care. We are all paying for it. Unfortunately, it is the most inefficient form of socialized health care. It does however; provide health care insurance companies with the largest profits. The new, single-payer, socialized health care should be paid for by people – _NOT_ by businesses. A flat–rate payroll tax that everyone pays will make people realize that there are no free lunches. This will make people more open to the limitations that must be placed on coverage. _Yes, even rationing!_ To think that we can afford unlimited health care coverage for everybody is nonsense. One more point, the Affordable Care Act was supposed to save the taxpayers $1 trillion over ten years. Part of those savings was attributable to an across the board cut in payments to health care providers that accept Medicare. An across the board 29% cut was supposed to take effect on January 1, 2012. Congress passed the "doctor fix" to nix this cut. Apparently Congress realized that cutting payments so dramatically would just force doctors to stop seeing Medicare patients. So where is that $1 trillion of savings going to come from?

11. Patient Protection and Affordable Care Act (aka: the Affordable Care Act, aka2: Obamacare)

Definition: Should the Affordable Care Act be repealed? Is it right that the government should ensure everyone has access to health care? Is it constitutionally correct to require an individual to purchase any product?

Far Left: See Medicare discussion. And, of course it is constitutionally correct to require people to purchase health care – they will inevitably need health care so they should pay for it.

Far Right: See Medicare discussion. And, it is not constitutionally correct to require an individual to purchase anything – including health care. Furthermore, once businesses have the choice of providing health care benefits, or paying an 8% payroll fine for not doing so – the businesses will elect to pay the 8% fine. Eight percent is much less than the cost of health care benefits so businesses will opt for the least expensive alternative. Then, all Americans will wind up on the government sponsored plan. This is how the Far Left plans on getting America to the single-payer, socialized health care that it really wants.

From the Middle: See Medicare discussion. And, the Supreme Court will make the correct call on the constitutionality of the issue. It appears as though they will strike it down. However, predictions of the Supreme Court are hard to make. If it is struck down – draft the socialized health care bill. The bill will be very simple. Everyone receives the basic benefits of Medicare and all employees (not employers) pay an 8% payroll tax for the privilege. Employers that currently pay for health care can either: 1) save the money and be more globally competitive, 2) give their employees a one-time 8% raise to offset the employees' new costs, or 3) provide the "add on coverage" that the more affluent seniors purchase today so that their employees can still enjoy the high-quality health care that they currently receive. Whatever – please, let us get beyond this issue.

12. Medicaid

See the Patient Protection and Affordable Care Act discussion.

13. European debt

Definition: Several countries in the Euro zone (i.e.: Portugal, Italy, Ireland, Greece and Spain – the so called PIGS) have national debts well over 100% of their gross domestic product. The interest payments on their debt are choking their governments' ability to stay current on their loan commitments (bond interest payments). As a result, the Euro zone partners have imposed strict austerity programs on these countries. These austerity programs have resulted in economic contraction, severe unemployment (25% in Spain) and riots in the streets of Athens (apparently people do not like being told at the last minute that their retirement age is five years later than they had been promised). Will the economic contraction in these countries impact the American economy? Are we on

21

a similar path to unbearable national debt? The International Monetary Fund has accumulated $430 billion dollars to help cushion the blow of any defaulting countries. Should the United States be contributing to this fund?

Far Left: Europe will be okay. They are taking care of themselves. We are America - the largest economy on the planet. There is no need to worry that we will become the next PIG.

Far Right: DING, DING, DING – this is big. We do not have to help Europe. They can take care of themselves. However, they will have to cut Greece loose. Greece will suffer dire consequences. AND, WE ARE ON THE SAME PATH. Our current policies have our national debt growing FOREVER. When debt grows forever, one day you cannot afford it anymore. Remember all those people that refinanced their homes over and over again (as if the homes were ATMs)? The refinancing money was used to take fancy vacations, purchase flashy cars, or pay for their kids' college education. Are there any homes in foreclosure in your neighborhood? So, let's keep spending money we do not have. It is easy, borrow from the Chinese, and then purchase their stuff with the money they lend us. This is insanity.

From the Middle: The Middle is with the Far Right on this one. Unfortunately, this is one of those crises that is beyond the next election cycle. Therefore, politicians do not want to deal with it. However, this is precisely _the issue_ that must lead us to change our politics. We cannot wait for the fear of the catastrophe that will happen tomorrow – it will be too late by then.

14. The National Debt

See European Debt discussion.

15. Religious Freedom

Definition: Where are the lines drawn between church and state? Can the government force any religious organization to fund activities that are diametrically opposed to their religious beliefs? This issue arose because a hospital run by the Catholic Church did not include birth control in its employees' health care benefits. President Obama got involved and announced that the Church did not have to pay for the benefit but that the health insurance company would provide it nonetheless. The Catholic Church was not pleased with the President interfering in their "religious" affairs.

Far Left: This is not about religious freedom – it is about women's rights. Specifically, it is about a woman's right to birth control. It is an example of how the Far Right is conducting a "war on women".

Far Right: Absolutely NOT! The government cannot force a religious organization to fund activities that are against its beliefs.

From the Middle: The line has to be drawn between church and state. If a religious organization enters the open marketplace and employs people from various faiths (or with no faith), they are in the public square. Therefore, the rules of the public square should apply – in this case pay for birth control. However, if the Church conducts only religious matters and requires employees to either be of their faith or know that they are expected to abide by the teachings of their faith – then they play by the Churches rules – not the public square rules.

16. War Against Religion

Definition: This issue is broader than the "Religious Freedom" issue discussed above. This is primarily a Christian issue. It appears to Christians that it is okay to display signs of faith in the public square as long as the faith is not Christian. For example, the phrase "Merry Christmas" has been replaced with "Happy Holidays".

Far Left: Christians should suck it up and yield to the minority faiths of our nation to better assimilate them into our culture.

Far Right: Our founding fathers created this nation based upon their Christian values. It is absolutely okay to adorn the public square with signs of the Christian faith. Most Americans are Christian. That is why there are more Christian signs than non-Christian signs. It is also the reason that Christmas is a national holiday.

From the Middle: All faiths, including Christian, should have the right to express their faith in the public square. Merry Christmas and Happy Holidays – and whatever specific holiday you want to wish merriment on – please do. Just, do _NOT_ infringe on the Christian's rights – or anyone else's rights.

17. Abortion

Definition: Abortions have been legal in the United States since the Supreme Court ruled on Roe vs. Wade in 1973. However, the basis of the decision was a woman's right to privacy. Ever since, there has been an on-going debate as to whether abortion should be outlawed as the murder of an unborn person. Should abortion be outlawed?

Far Left: No, the Supreme Court got it right and this is just another example of the Far Right's war on women.

Far Right: Absolutely it should be outlawed. It is murder.

From the Middle: This is not a war on women. The percentage of Americans that favor abortion has been slowly declining for years to the point that today, more than 50% of Americans believe that abortion should be outlawed. This is a debate that is being settled through public discourse that needs to continue. It should not be a campaign issue at this time. In the near future, it should be addressed through referendums on state ballets. The public needs to decide this issue – not politicians.

18. Women Earn $0.77 for Every $1.00 Men Earn

Definition: Self explanatory.

Far Left: This is an example of how poorly women are treated in our male dominated society. It is the intentional policies of the Republican Party that allow this inequity to continue.

Far Right: It is true that women earn less than men. In cases where women are doing the exact same job as a man – this is wrong. There are laws on the books that already prohibit such conditions. In general, women earn less due to the fact that they bear the majority of the child-raising responsibilities in our society. Whereas most men do not take a break from their careers (sometimes for several years) to raise their children, many women do. This results in women losing ground in rising up the ranks of corporate America. This is why women, on average, earn less than men.

From the Middle: We agree with the far right on this one. However, there are other factors involved that are culturally based. Women dominate our care-giving fields of occupation. Care-giving (child and elderly) are extremely important jobs. However, our society does not pay those jobs commensurate with their value. Men dominate the heavy, unskilled labor jobs like garbage collection. There is nothing wrong with being a garbage collector. But why does a garbage collector make $60K a year while a child day-care worker makes $20K? This issue is more about our value system than either party's public policy positions.

19. Paul Ryan's Proposed Budget

Definition: Paul Ryan is a congressman from the state of Wisconsin. He has introduced a bill in Congress to establish a national budget (which is constitutionally required of both Congress and the Senate). Congressman Ryan's budget bill has been passed by the Republican controlled Congress but will not even be brought to the floor of the Senate. The Senate has not passed a budget for over three years. Congressman Ryan's budget actually cuts our national debt by $3 trillion over the next ten years. However, to achieve this debt reduction, Congressman Ryan includes spending cuts to some of our entitlement programs. Child-care for low-income, working mothers is one such cut. There are cuts to several of our social net expenditures.

Far Left: This is horrible, right-wing, social reengineering (thank you Mr. Gingrich for providing this tag line). It demonstrates the lack of compassion that the Far Right has towards those less fortunate among us. None of these cuts can be tolerated. This is another example of the "war on women". Cutting low-income mothers' child-care support is despicable.

Far Right: This is a great budget. It starts to bring our fiscal house to order.

<u>From the Middle</u>: This is a great first step. Just as the Far Right has to compromise on tax increases, the Far Left has to compromise on spending cuts. Finally someone has put down on paper a starting point for negotiations. Congress (including the Senate) should actually debate this budget and collaborate on something that would give Americans what is desperately needed – some leadership!

20. War on Woman

<u>Definition</u>: The debates over abortion, contraception, women's pay, and Congressman Ryan's budget proposal have been characterized by the Far Left as a "war on women". And, just to pile on - the Republican led Congress held hearings on whether or not the government had the right to require the Catholic Church to provide birth control. The panel of experts that the Republicans called upon consisted of only men – *no woman*.

<u>Far Left</u>: It is true. The Far Right wants women to stay in the dark ages. Not including women when debating birth control is a demonstration of the Far Right's lack of sensitivity to women issues.

<u>Far Right</u>: This is ridiculous. We will not pay for condoms for men either. (That last sentence was just a little humor to perk the readers up. However, it is true. Insurance companies do not pay for condoms.)

<u>From the Middle</u>: There is no issue here to discuss. Abortion and birth control benefits are separate issues that happen to affect woman more than men. However, they do affect men. Women's pay versus men is an issue but it is not due to either party's policies. Rather, it is due to our cultural value system. Congressman Ryan's budget does cut some programs that affect women. But it also cuts into

Social Security, Medicare and many other social safety-net programs. Women were not specifically targeted. Furthermore, we must make some spending cuts.

21. No Child Left Behind

Definition: The Bush administration established regulations that require children to be tested using standardized tests. Schools that continually fail to educate their children (based on the test results) are eventually taken over by the state to better provide the education that all our children deserve.

Far Left: Testing is not an accurate measure of a school's performance. Standardized testing should be abandoned.

Far Right: Standardized testing is a good measure. Schools that do not measure up should be held accountable. Teacher unions that oppose testing need to get on board. Education is about the children - not the teachers. Failing schools should be reorganized.

From the Middle: We are with the Far Right on this one - with one caveat. The testing should not be limited to reading, writing and arithmetic. Testing should measure the totality of our children's' development. The current standardized testing has resulted in cuts to the arts, music and cultural lessons that our children received in the past. America's greatness is in our creativity. We should not allow ourselves to become a nation of robots that can recite multiplication tables.

22. Everyone Should Go to College

Definition: Should everyone go to college, and why does it cost so much? The unemployment rate for people with a college education is much lower than the population in general. College educated people earn higher wages than non-college educated people. Do we all need to be college educated in order to maintain our economic competitiveness in the global economy?

<u>Far Left</u>: We do need more college educated people to be competitive in the global economy because the global economy is more knowledge-based than ever before. Also, many of our traditional manufacturing jobs have been automated and now require a college education to run the machinery. However, we also need skilled tradesmen and unskilled labor to do all the work that needs to be done in America.

<u>Far Right</u>: Ditto

<u>From the Middle</u>: Ditto. Why has this issue been debated? Everybody seems to agree to the same principles. However, nobody is discussing why college costs so much. Maybe it is because college professors are paid too much. Maybe it is poor management by college administrators. Maybe it is just poor consumer choice. Everybody wants to have the college name with the most prestige on their diploma. We should leverage more of our community colleges for the foundation courses and have our children (young adults) attend the expensive colleges for the last two years. That would save families a lot of money – and maybe even get those prestigious colleges to start competing with lower tuitions.

23. NASA

<u>Definition</u>: NASA's budget has been severely cut. Should we continue to fund any space exploration? Should we let private enterprise decide if there is a demand for space travel, exploration, or commercial use?

Far Left: We cannot afford any of it. Let private industry take it over.

Far Right: We have to continue space exploration for military purposes.

From the Middle: We agree with the Far Right for military purposes and with the Far Left on private involvement for profit. There are many profit motives already in place for private sector space exploration. For example, shooting a satellite up that will provide cell phone service, television broadcasting, weather monitoring, Google maps, etc...

24. Research & Development in General

Definition: Should the government fund R&D?

Far Left: Absolutely. The government has to provide research dollars for alternative fuels and for new sciences that are not understood by the marketplace as potential new sources of economic growth.

Far Right: Absolutely not. Let the private sector make their own investments and reap the rewards from them.

From the Middle: We agree with the Far Left but we have to be very prudent on how much money we spend and let scientists (not Congress) make the decisions on where the money should be spent.

25. Qualifications to be President

Definition: Personal attacks against a candidate's religion or lack thereof, their experience, their moral character, etc. always come up during campaigns. Governor Romney has the advantages of business experience and job creation. He also has the disadvantage of his company, Bain Capital, having been involved in the shuttering of some businesses – which created layoffs. President Obama was elected with no executive experience, but he now has four years of such experience. What are the qualifications to be the President?

<u>Far Left</u>: Governor Romney has a track record of laying people off. He even stated that he likes to fire people. (This comment was taken out of context with regard to Governor Romney discussing the firing of businesses that provide poor service. Governor Romney was commenting on how competition makes goods and services better.)

<u>Far Right</u>: President Obama's lack of executive experience has been evident in the many blunders of his first term. In addition, his affiliation with Reverend White for over twenty years demonstrates that his values are not consistent with the majority of Americans.

<u>From the Middle</u>: The specific personal attacks made by the Far Left and Far Right are meaningless. Governor Romney and President Obama are very qualified candidates. However, this is a big issue – not just for the president but for all of our elected leaders. We need statesmen. We need the rare individual that does not get rankled by the twenty-four by seven news cycle and the attacks against their possible defection from the staunch party-line. The main qualification that we believe in is that the candidate has <u>*NOT*</u> signed any pledges to never raise taxes (or any other pledge). How can someone effectively develop new policy (in a bi-partisan manner) after they have committed to a no-compromise position? This matter will be more fully discussed in "The Statesmen" chapter.

26. Green Energy

<u>Definition</u>: This is not an issue regarding the use of green energy. Everybody would be for green energy if it were affordable and could provide enough energy. This is an

issue that came up because of the Solyndra scandal. Solyndra was a company that was provided with a $500 million stimulus package, government guaranteed loan. Unfortunately, Solyndra was allowed to restructure the terms of the loan (putting the government loan in second place in the event of a default) and guess what happened? Solyndra filed for bankruptcy a few months after the government restructured its loan. We taxpayers got stuck for the $500 million.

Far Left: See the Research and Development in General discussion.

Far Right: See the Research and Development in General discussion. But, let us not miss the opportunity to point out the incompetence of the current administration.

From the Middle: See the Research and Development in General discussion. And, the government did not have a 100% score in picking winners while doling out the stimulus money. Does anyone ever score a 100%? The lesson that should be learned here is that the government cannot prudently spend $787 billion in two years. The stimulus spending was necessary. But, it should have been less, or it should have been spent over a longer period of time. More time would have allowed more prudent decisions on where to spend the money. Back to Solyndra, the government allowed the debt to be restructured because it knew Solyndra was failing and needed more money. By restructuring the debt, Solyndra was able to procure some private investment funding. Unfortunately, it was not enough and Solyndra failed. We were not going to get our money back whether we allowed Solyndra to restructure the loan or not.

27. Gas Prices

Definition: Gas prices have hit $4.00 per gallon. Is there anything that can be done to get them back to a reasonable price?

Far Left: Let them go higher. Fossil fuels cause green house gases and are creating global warming. The higher the gas prices, the more incentive there is for people to shift to alternative, green sources of energy.

Far Right: Build the pipeline from Canada to Texas. Drill for more oil in the United States. Extract more natural gas here at home. Develop clean coal technologies. Become completely self-sufficient in our energy needs.

From the Middle: We agree with the Far Right on this one. We truly need an "all of the above" approach. Furthermore, we need to require oil companies that are drilling on leased land from the government to sell that oil in the United States at controlled prices (cost plus a reasonable profit). We should not allow oil companies to sell OUR oil on the world market at the world prices. It is our oil! It would also be very nice to stop sending all of our money to countries that we cannot trust.

28. Oil Pipelines

Definition: Should we build (or actually expand) an oil pipeline from Canada to Texas? This issue is separated from the "Gas Prices" issue discussed above for one reason – it is the environmentalists that have held up this project. So even though it can help gas prices, there is another issue to be dealt with – can we do anything without delays or outright stoppages due to environmental concerns? Off shore drilling is another example of this issue.

<u>Far Left</u>: Cannot do it – too environmentally risky.

<u>Far Right</u>: Have to do it for our national security and economic stability. We depend too much on foreign oil. Furthermore, we have proven technology. We can do it with virtually no risk to the environment.

<u>From the Middle</u>: Well, we did have the BP oil spill in the Gulf of Mexico so we should at least recognize that there are risks. However, is it responsible of us to import as much oil as we do? Do the countries that are drilling for that oil *NOT* take environmental risks? Is the environment *NOT* a global concern? Our government will provide better oversight of environmental protection than those foreign counties. When you consider the economic and environmental issues, it is irresponsible not to build the pipeline – or to drill off shore. The Chinese are drilling off the coast of Cuba. That is pretty close to the United States. What level of safety measures do you think they employ?

29. Drill Baby Drill

See the Oil Pipeline discussion.

30. Global Warming

<u>Definition</u>: Scientific measurement of the planet's temperature has shown that the temperature has increased over the past hundred years (although it appears as though it has not been rising the past few years). Many scientists believe that the burning of carbon based fossil fuels have caused this temperature rise. The carbon dioxide byproduct of burning fossil fuels rises in the atmosphere and causes a "green house" effect. This means that the carbon dioxide allows the energy of the sun to pass through and then traps that energy inside the planet's environment.

Far Left: This is real and we should stop burning fossil fuels. Green energy alternatives must be employed now. Furthermore, we should pass "cap and trade" legislation. This will stop us from increasing the amount of carbon dioxide we produce. If someone is not making carbon dioxide today but wants to make it in the future, they will have to purchase "credits" from somebody that is burning fossil fuels and making carbon dioxide today. This will force businesses to become more efficient and/or switch to green energy.

Far Right: There is no scientific proof that man is creating this condition. There is no need to change our energy menu. Also, "cap and trade" is like shooting ourselves in the foot. How can we compete in the world market if we charge our businesses fees that other countries do not charge their businesses?

From the Middle: Something is happening. Putting a lot of bad stuff into the environment is not a good idea for long term sustainability. Maybe the global warming is not man made – but it probably is. In either case, we do not want to take any chances. We should invest in alternative fuel development. We should also invest some of our research and development money in *global warming mitigation* (rather than investing all of our R&D funds in global warming prevention through green energy). We cannot make an immediate change to the types of energy we consume. That is impossible and it is not yet warranted. We need to work this issue at the global level. If we voluntarily start spending more on energy than the rest of the world, how are we going to be able to sell any of our products? Let's get a global plan of action so we are prepared for the future. If it is cap and trade, let it be cap and trade at the global level.

31. Energy in General

See the discussions on: 1) Green Energy, 2) Gas Prices, 3) Oil Pipeline, 4) Drill Baby Drill, and 5) Global Warming.

32. The Environment in General

See the Oil Pipeline and Global Warming discussions.

33. Gay Rights

Definition: Should gay and lesbian people be allowed to get married?

Far Left: Absolutely!

Far Right: Absolutely NOT!

From the Middle: This issue has gotten old. Let's bury it. Gay and lesbian people deserve every right that the rest of society has. In fact, if the issue from the Far Right is that the bible defines marriage as the joining of a man and a woman – then this is a religious issue, *NOT* a public policy issue. Therefore, nobody should get a government issued marriage license. Everyone should get a civil union license from the government. If anyone wants to get married, they should go to their place of worship. We also do not buy the argument that this is a state issue. The Supreme Court will one day hear the case of a united gay couple. The couple will have been united in one state (where such unions are legal) and then moved to a state where civil unions are not legal. The couple will sue to have their civil union privileges granted in their new state of residency. Then it will become a federal matter. So let us solve the problem right now – civil unions for all!

34. Immigration

Definition: Should we build a fence? Should we deport eleven million people? Should we grant amnesty? Should we build a "pathway to citizenship"? Should we pay for immigrants' college tuitions? To some people, this is very personal and very, very scary.

Far Left: Amnesty for all.

Far Right: Build a fence, round up all eleven million and deport them.

From the Middle: We need to be practical. We are never going to round up eleven million people. Build a fence and stop the problem from growing. Then, let everyone register as legal alien residents. Once that is done, enforce our immigration laws, and deport anybody that breaks them. For legal alien residents, they need to pay taxes and be eligible for government benefits like the rest of the population. Furthermore, since we are not going to round them up and deport them, of course we should establish a path to citizenship for the registered legal aliens. Do we really want eleven million people, who have not pledged their allegiance to the United States of America, living among us? Back to the fence, we really could implement this plan without the fence – so we should not use the excuse of constructing delays to stop us from moving forward.

35. Reverse Discrimination

Definition: Should we keep affirmative action laws alive or have we reached the point where the unfair practices of the past have been counter balanced by the existing affirmative action laws so that we no longer need them?

<u>Far Left</u>: They are still needed.

<u>Far Right</u>: They have accomplished what they were intended to accomplish. It is time to move on.

<u>From the Middle</u>: We are with the Far Left on this one. Anyone that rides through an inner-city area of our nation has to realize that we have not yet done enough. However, we need to refocus our affirmative action laws. The current laws provide assistance to those that know how to use the laws. Those that need the most help have no idea that affirmative action laws even exist. Quotas for admissions into colleges or for corporate managerial positions are no longer needed. The affluent minority individuals have already arrived. It was thought that the mere existence of minorities in positions of esteem would inspire all minorities to pull themselves up by the bootstraps. Well, the examples are now everywhere and the inner-city population still has a culture all of its own. The quota system we use today is outdated. What is needed is quotas on how many entry level minorities are employed *NOT* how many are in the bosses office. We need to assimilate the inner-city into our broader society. If we do not, we will continue to be afraid of driving through the streets of our cities forever. Leadership from our minority populations is also in dire need. Nobody should ever be misled into believing that America does not provide opportunity for everybody. Unfortunately, many in our lower socioeconomic class believe this. Even worse, many of them believe that they are targeted for punishment by society. This unfounded belief system has resulted in some people adopting a "no snitch" policy. The "no snitch" policy is intended to keep the broader society away from those that believe they are victims. Unfortunately, it just further exacerbates the crime rates in

the areas where such belief systems exist. Leaders that proliferate this "victim" mentality need to go away.

36. Race Relations

Definition: We are now twenty years after the Rodney King riots of Los Angeles, and the Sanford Florida shooting of a young African American has renewed racial tensions in the United States.

Far Left: Race relations are as bad today as they were twenty years ago.

Far Right: Race relations are much better today than twenty years ago. The African American leaders (specifically Al Sharpton) and the media have irresponsibly played this current tragedy into a racial issue. There are still a few racists in our society – and there always will be. In general, we have come a long way. We may not be all the way to where we should be on racial matters – but we are very close – and getting better every day.

From the Middle: We thought the election of the country's first African American president was going to be the end of racial tension in America. Unfortunately, that is not the case. This is not the President's fault. It is the fault of the local, minority leaders (or the lack thereof). As discussed in the "Affirmative Action" issue immediately preceding this discussion; the inner-city of America is still a frightening place to visit. There is a culture of mistrust among many of our minority youth that is misplaced. We need minority leaders to shine a light on this problem. With that said, race relations are much better than they were twenty years ago. We agree with the Far Right's view of the irresponsible actions of the media. The Florida criminal case needs to be very transparent so that all Americans see how our justice system works and can have faith in the eventual outcome – whichever way the verdict falls. We must also remind everyone that our system of justice (for better or worse – and it is better) is innocent until proven guilty. Our children are much blinder to race than we older Americans. In this, we should see that we have come a long way and are continuing in the right direction. The African American community desperately needs more leaders that see the world as it truly is – and get rid of the Al Sharptons.

37. Campaign Funding Part I

Definition: In 2010, the US Federal District Court of Washington DC ruled in the "SpeechNow.org" case that Super PACs (Political Action Committees) have the right to collect donations of any size and, therefore, spend unlimited amounts of money during political campaigns. As a result, there are Democratic and Republican super PACS that blast the air waves with negative advertisements and distorted facts. The super PACs are completely separate from the candidate's campaign team. In fact, the laws require that the candidates have no communication with the super PACs at all.

Far Left: No changes are needed, it is working well.

Far Right: No changes are needed, it is working well.

From the Middle: Ban the super PACs. Their billions of dollars – if not coordinated with the candidate's campaign – certainly appear to be coordinated. These super PACs allow the candidate to stay above the fray of negative campaigning because their surrogate Super PAC fills that role. The amount of money that is now available for negative campaigning has distorted most Americans' view of reality. Some people actually come to despise the candidate from "the other team" because of all this negativity. Worse yet, some Americans come to despise other civilians that support "the other team". The truth of the matter is that the candidates from both parties are good, honest people – or they would not have attained the position of being a candidate (Presidential, Senatorial, or Congressional). More on this issue is covered in the issue of "Money's Corruption of Our Political Process".

38. Campaign Funding Part II

Definition: Each candidate running for president has to declare whether he or she will accept public funding. If public funding is accepted, the amount that the candidate can spend on their campaign is limited. If they reject public funding of their campaign, the candidate can spend as much money as they can raise. The public funding option is never chosen.

Far Left: No changes are needed, it is working well.

Far Right: No changes are needed, it is working well.

From the Middle: Require all candidates to use public funds and limit their campaign spending. The New York Times recently wrote an article about Australia and New Zealand. In those countries, everyone is required to vote – or be fined. Therefore, there is less campaigning to the "base" of the candidate's party and more campaigning to the populace in general – which means much less "Far Left" and "Far Right" rhetoric. They also limit the time allowed for the campaign. We should follow their lead. The long duration of our campaigns, coupled with the vast quantity of negativity we spew, only causes more division. The division makes it harder for anything to be accomplished once the elections are over. Wait a minute. They are never over. As soon as the 2012 election is over, the media will be talking about 2016 – who do you think will run?

39. Money's Corruption of the Political Process

Definition: First of all – this is not an issue being debated during this election campaign season. It is included here because, even though it is not being discussed, it is a huge problem. It is closely related to the Super PAC discussion of the above campaign funding issue but it is broader. The amount of spending by lobbyists who are sponsored by industry groups, individual companies, unions and even wealthy individual Americans has dramatically changed the way politics are conducted. In the early days of the United States, our elected leaders listened to their constituents to help them understand the issues of the day and to develop public policies to address those issues. Nowadays, the individual voter gets to cast their vole in an "American Idol" style competition (the election). Following the election, ordinary citizens have no say until the next election. The business of the elected office holder is influenced by lobbyists that round up big-money donators – _NOT_ by the office holder's constituents. When the Affordable Care Act was being debated, it was the health insurance companies' lobbyists that gained access to our elected leaders. The poor-old-little-American-schmuck had hardly a say. What we ended up with was a 2,700 page bill that benefited the health insurance companies but did little to solve America's health care problems. Another blatant example of this was the Bush Medicare Prescription Drug Plan. The drug companies were allowed to write large pieces of the law. We ended up with a bill that prevented the largest consumer of prescription drugs in the world (the US government) to _NOT_ be allowed to shop for the least expensive sources of those drugs. The special-interest groups influence all of our legislation – and, push the little-guy's opinion out of the picture. The politicians have allowed this "big-money" corruption to occur for one reason: self-survival. If one office holder does it, he or she gains the advantage of money pouring into their re-election campaign fund (or into their surrogate Super PAC fund). Therefore, to remain competitive, all office holders kowtow to the lobbyists. That way, they can raise as much money as the other guys. As a result, special-interest groups now dominate our public policy making – _NOT_ the true interests of the populace.

Far Left: This is the sad reality of today's political landscape. We do not like it, but we have no choice but to play by the rules of this game. If not, we will become extinct. And, even with the "big-money" problem – we are ultimately accountable to our constituents for re-election.

Far Right: This is the sad reality of today's political landscape. We do not like it, but we have no choice but to play by the rules of this game. If not, we will become extinct. And, even with the "big-money" problem – we are ultimately accountable to our constituents for re-election.

From the Middle: The big-money helps spin any candidate's message. Big-money is also used to distort any opponent's record. This spin-doctoring makes it very difficult for the little guy to actually know if his elected representative is working for him or for a special-interest group. Therefore, the claim of being held accountable to constituents in the next election does not hold water. The truth of the matter is that the Far Left is okay with George Soros spending millions of dollars to make the Far Right appear to be Looney tunes. Similarly, the Far Right is okay with the Koch Brothers spending millions of dollars to make the Far Left appear to be Looney tunes. However, both the Far Left and the Far Right are aware that they have allowed our system to be corrupted. Unfortunately, neither can find a way out of this corruption. This is a very, very sad reality. A grass roots effort to overcome this system of political corruption is needed. However, the big-money machines that gain advantage from this system have too many resources. They would most likely squash any grass roots movement. The only way to overcome this corruption of American politics is for statesmanship to return to Washington. A full chapter of this book is devoted to "The Statesman" (gender neutral). It would be refreshing to see public debate centered on what is good for the populace - rather than what is good for some particular special interest group with deep pockets. The little guy believes that he or she has lost their voice in their own country.

40. The Inequity of Wealth in America

Definition: The Occupy Wall Street Movement has heightened Americans' awareness that there is a huge divide among the "haves" and "have-nots". The Occupy Wall Street Movement claims that the top 1% has the majority of wealth in America and that the remaining 99% are suffering as a result.

Far Left: The Occupy Wall Street people are correct. The disparity in wealth among the "haves" and "have-nots" is larger today than it has ever been. While the fat-cats have not felt the effects of the economic troubles, the little guy has been suffering terribly. We must raise taxes on the wealthiest among us and redistribute that wealth to the most unfortunate among us.

Far Right: This is America. We are the land of opportunity. If someone has the ability to earn a fortune, they have every right to do so. This is what makes America great. Don't the 99% aspire to become a part of the 1%? Of course they do. We should not lose sight of the fact that when a rich person has economic struggles, it is the little guy that suffers. When the rich person cannot afford their second or third home, it is the carpenters, plumbers and electricians that lose work.

From the Middle: America is about opportunity. It allows those from humble beginnings to become wealthy through hard work and good fortune. We do not ever wish to see this change. However, the disparity between the "haves" and "have-nots" is larger than it has ever been. We are not sure if this is a problem, or a symptom of another problem – *greed*. We do believe that the banking crisis had its origins in greed. There is a distinction between greed and profit motive. Profit motive is a positive thing that encourages competition on a fair playing field. Greed is when one knowingly takes advantage of another. Brokers knowingly peddled mortgages to people that did not understand the terms, nor had the ability to abide by those terms. The brokers then sold the mortgages to banks. The banks then bundled them into "mortgage backed securities". Then the banks, developed "credit default swaps" and "synthetic credit default swaps" to make more money off the exploitation of the poor mortgage holder.

The profit motive plays itself out in the exercise of capitalism. This is a good thing – as long as regulation maintains a level playing field. In the long term, the profit motive will benefit all the peoples of the world. However, in the interim, it will hurt Americans. The profit motive leads to goods being manufactured where labor is available and cheap (i.e.: China and Mexico). Those products are then sold to Americans - the same Americans that have been put out of work by the "offshore" manufacturing. We understand that this is capitalism at work and we fully support capitalism. We just think a little compassion could be coupled with capitalism. Such a coupling could go a long way to helping America. We should encourage manufacturers to produce goods in America. So, if a profit can still be had while manufacturing in America – please do so. As consumers, if we chose to pay a few extra dollars for the "Made in America" label – we will be doing our part.

As an aside, it seems as though this issue and the previous issue – "Money's Corruption of the Political Process" go hand-in-hand. The corruption by the special interest groups have led to regulation (or the lack of regulation, and even the lack of enforcement) that enables greed – rather than the profit motive. Has it been mentioned that those bankers should go to jail? Yes, it is the combination of these two issues that leave the little guy feeling like he is at a disadvantage. The Occupy Wall Street movement missed the opportunity of defining their issue – it has just been defined. The bankers are just an example; the issue is the corruption in our politics that has created an unfair playing field. The little guy does not feel as though his or her voice is heard – because it is not heard. To the Occupy Wall Street movement: please move your campsite from Wall Street to K Street (K Street in Washington DC is where most of the lobbyists have their offices).

41. Apologies

Definition: President Obama has apologized to the Islamic world for the United States not being (in the past) understanding of their world view – and for America making unilateral decisions that impact other countries.

Far Left: Apologizing is good in that it rebuilds strained relationships.

Far Right: Apologizing should never be done because it diminishes the respect that the United States deserves. The United States is _the_ world power that provides a beacon of hope to the world. Our past actions have been towards the goal of making the world a better place. Unfortunately, we do not have unlimited resources. Sometimes, we did not act when we may have been able to do good. We have to consider our national interests as well as the interests of human rights when we make decisions.

From the Middle: We agree with the Far Right on this one. We also believe that we need to lean on our NATO partners for more support when we do take action to make the world a better place. It was great to see France step up to the plate and take charge of the Libyan revolution. We must establish the expectations that our NATO partners do more of that. We are good people, but we cannot afford to be the only policemen in the world.

42. War on Terror

Definition: Ever since 9/11/2001, America has been engaged in a global war against terrorism. Originally, the war was primarily against Al Queda. There has been so much success in dismantling Al Queda's organization that the war is now viewed more broadly as against any organization or person that intends to inflict harm on America. The Al Queda of Bin Laden no longer exists. The new Al Queda is based in Yemen and is referred to as the AQAP (Al Queda in the Arabian Peninsula). AQAP may develop the same organizational skills that Bin Laden's Al

Queda possessed. However, right now it appears as though our most likely threat will come from the "lone-wolf" that is the hardest to identify and stop.

Far Left: Keep on fighting, but do not ever invade another country in the name of "war on terror" again (i.e.: Iraq, Afghanistan). When we do find foreign operatives planning or working on the execution of a terrorist plot against America – use drones and/or special forces to eliminate them. Some on the Far Left believe that this is unconstitutional – especially when we are killing an American civilian in this manner (as was done in a strike in Yemen). However, the majority of the Left believe that with enough proof against the target – this is an appropriate measure.

Far Right: We actually agree with the Far Left on this one.

From the Middle: This appears to be the one issue where everyone agrees.

43. Russia, Communism, and Iraq

Definition: This issue is listed here for illustration only. Not too long ago these matters dominated our dialog. They are now non-issues. The fact that they are non-issues speaks volumes about how the world has changed.

Iraq cost us thousands of lives and a trillion dollars and it is though we do not even care about it anymore. It is not something we even think about. If Iran has its way, it will take over Iraq as a starting point to taking over the entire Middle-East. Iran is a serious issue that is discussed separately.

Communism appears to only be living in Cuba these days. Who knows if that will continue after Fidel Castro dies? The past kings of communism (Russia and China) now practice capitalism. It may involve a lot of state-run capitalistic companies – but it is capitalism. It is hard to imagine that any large country will experiment with communism again. The totalitarianism that seemed to always accompany communism still exists. It will probably exist somewhere on the planet forever. However, the internet has made it much more difficult for this form of government to survive. The totalitarianism of China and Russia will someday go the way of communism.

A state-run capitalistic company is a real issue that is not being discussed. With most of the new oil well-heads being drilled in foreign countries, capitalistic companies must present a compelling reason for the local government to allow them to drill holes in their land (or sea bottom). American companies promise better financial returns than the state-run capitalistic companies can deliver. However, these state-run companies (from China and Russia) can also throw in an arms deal that the local dictator may see as a more valuable commodity than wealth for his or her people.

Russia is a nuisance because it retains its veto power on the Security Council of the United Nations. But, Russia is no longer a threat to the United States. The cold war that lasted forty-six years is over. America's new archrival is China. The world has changed much in the past decade. The nuisance of Russia is discussed in the issue of "The United Nations". China has its own issue discussion.

Since there is no issue here – there will be no Far Left, Far Right or Middle of the Road positions listed.

An issue that will rise after this book is released is President Obama's remarks made to Russian President Medvedev that he thought were made in private. President Obama told President Medvedev to inform Russia's President Elect (Vladimir Putin) to hold off on any demands regarding America's missile defense system. President Obama told the Russians that he would have more "flexibility" to negotiate with them after the elections. President Obama was not aware that there was an open microphone when he made those remarks. It is obvious that there will be a television commercial of these remarks aired thousands of times during the campaign (after the party conventions). Whether this turns out to be a big issue will depend on how President Obama responds to the attacks that have yet to be fired.

The "flexibility" statement has the potential to unleash a powerful emotion in the American electorate – mistrust of its government. This emotion was stirred when Congress used a budgeting loop-hole called "reconciliation" to pass the Affordable Care Act. Most Americans did not support the Affordable Care Act but Congress passed it anyway – using the inappropriate tactic (reconciliation). If Americans believe that President Obama is playing fast and loose with his Presidential authority, he will pay a heavy price. Keep an eye on how this issue plays itself out.

A footnote must be added to remain fair on this topic of reconciliation. Both Bush tax cuts and the Bush Medicare prescription law were passed using the reconciliation provision. It was not correct to use reconciliation for those pieces of legislation either. Whereas the Far Left did not lampoon the Far Right for its usage of the reconciliation provision, the Far Right did. They were very adept at spinning the use of reconciliation for the Affordable Care Act as a misuse of the Senate rules. The Far Right was correct, it was a misuse of the Senate rules – but the far Right also has egg on its face.

44. The Middle East

Definition: Israel and its Arab neighbors have been in conflict ever since Israel was founded as a nation in 1947. Egypt is the only Arab state to have signed a peace treaty with Israel. With the overthrow of the Egyptian government, many in Egypt are calling for an end to that peace treaty. The Palestinians have long wished to be recognized as a sovereign state. Much of the radical Islamist terror in the world is targeted at either Israel or America for supporting Israel. Why can't this issue be resolved? This issue is so complex that only the surface can be scratched in the format of this book.

Far Left: Israel should start negotiations with Palestinians using the borders of Israel that were in place before the six-day war of 1967. Israel should stop all West Bank settlement development as a precondition for peace talks with the Palestinians.

Far Right: Israel should not give an inch. We must support them with whatever they believe is necessary to protect them. Israel is the only true democracy in the region of the world where we have strategic interests (oil).

From the Middle: This is one of those impossible issues. Israel should stop further settlement in the West Bank. The pre-1967 border starting point will never work for Israel. We cannot support Israel with whatever they want. We have to let them know that for us to be supportive, they have to be willing to give a few inches to the Palestinians. The two-state (Israel and Palestine) solution is the only solution that will bring peace to this region of the world. We should also be focusing a lot of diplomacy on Turkey. Turkey is likely to become the (non-Israel) regional power, and their influence will have an enormous impact on the Arab world. As has been the case since the end of World War II, this region is the powder keg that could ignite World War III. With Pakistan having nuclear bombs and an apparently undisciplined government, the powder keg has become more threatening. With Iran on its way to having nuclear weapons and having called for the obliteration of Israel – we are at a very scary point in history.

45. Afghanistan

Definition: Have we anything left to accomplish here? Should we stay or should we go?

Far Left: We got Bin Laden, let's get out of Dodge.

Far Right: We should stay until the mission is accomplished (what is that mission?). If we leave now the nation-building that we have accomplished will all be lost.

From the Middle: We are with the Far Left on this one. How much are we spending here? It has become very clear that nation-building in Afghanistan is not a practical outcome. Vice President Biden was correct when he advocated against the troop surge. His call for a smaller footprint in Afghanistan with more emphasis on special operation forces and drones would have been better. (Note: The author did not agree with Vice President Biden at the time. Hindsight is 20/20. At least the author admits when he is wrong. We need more of that from our leaders. Changing positions as a result of learning is not flip-flopping.)

46. Iran

Definition: Iran has blatantly violated its international treaties to NOT proliferate nuclear weapons. They are very close to having a nuclear bomb. They already have the long range rockets needed to send bombs into Israel. Their president has publically stated that Israel should be obliterated off the face of the planet. Should Israel, the United States, or both of us, bomb Iran before they become too radioactive? Will sanctions stop Iran from going nuclear? Will Iran really shut down the Straits of Hormuz (through which 20% of the world's oil flows) if they get bombed? Will Iran bomb the entire oil infrastructure in the Middle-East (which happens to be where the world gets most of its oil)? Does Iran have plans to dominate the Middle-East? This is a scary one.

Far Left: Let them have nuclear bombs. They are rational people and will not use them to bomb Israel. Furthermore, can you blame them for wanting to have nuclear weapons? Countries that have nuclear weapons do not worry about the United States bombing them (e.g.: North Korea). Countries that do not have nuclear weapons do worry about the United States bombing them (e.g.: Libya). Iran does not have ambitions of dominating the Middle-East.

Far Right: Let's not wait for Israel to bomb Iran. Let's do it ourselves today. If we wait any longer we will not be able to stop them from going nuclear. Iran does plan on dominating the Middle-East. They have already established Lebanon as a puppet state. They are now working on taking control of Iraq. If they are successful in taking control of Iraq, they will move on to their next victim. After all the blood and treasure we lost in Iraq, we should do something to stop Iran. Sanctions will never work because Russia and China continue to do business with Iran.

From the Middle: Let's act at the last possible moment and work every other non-military solution to its maximum effect before *thinking* about another war. If Israel goes in without us – that is their call (and it would probably be the correct call). Israel took care of Iraq and Syria's nuclear ambitions with military strikes, and the world is a better place for it. However, if Israel does pull the trigger, we need to be ready to defend the entire Middle-East region. In fact, defending the Middle-East, dismantling the Iranian military without invading their country and *NOT* rebuilding Iran may be just what the United States needs to regain its respect as *the* global military power. All this failed nation building has diminished our world standing. Let's walk softly but carry a big stick – and let the world know we can swing that stick. With that said, let us all pray that none of this happens.

47. The Arab Spring

Definition: Iran, Tunisia, Egypt, Libya, Yemen, Bahrain, and Syria have seen the populace rise up against oppression and, in some cases, overthrow dictators. However, the aftermath has left some of these countries being taken over by radical Islamists. Should the United States have any role in supporting these uprisings – or a role in tampering them down? We helped the Libyans overthrow Gaddafi and allowed the Bahrain uprising to be squashed (of course our navy has a fleet docked there so we like their leaders).

Far Left: Never interfere with the internal matters of a legitimate state. However, if a state's legitimacy has been lost due to its human rights violations (e.g.: Syria) then by all means, bring sanctions against the illegitimate government and announce to the world that we support the opposition – but do not provide any real support to the opposition.

<u>Far Right</u>: Same as the Far Left – but, on a case by case situation, evaluate the possibility for, and use military intervention to help the opposition.

<u>From the Middle</u>: Make sure that any opposition groups we support are good people. Henry Kissinger stated that the people who start revolutions are usually not the same people that end the revolutions (meaning that somebody else steps in after the dictator has been overthrown and fills the leadership void). Therefore, we have no idea who will be in charge when the revolutions end. But, if we state that we are for the good guys up front – the people of the involved nation will respect us. Hopefully, the nation will eventually have the freedoms we enjoy. Once a country has true freedom – the government becomes a representation of its people. We must make rational decisions on who we are going to support and who we are not going to support and communicate those decisions to the world community. We should have communicated our support for the Iranian uprising. At that time, we already believed that the Iranian government was rogue (not legitimate) for both its pursuit of nuclear weapons and its brutal crackdown on the populace uprising. We agree to evaluate military options on a case by case scenario – but we do not want to engage in any nation-building – so the military option can only be with our NATO partners – like in Libya.

48. Military

Definition: Spending cuts are necessary if we ever want to get our fiscal house in order. Should the military be spared the cutting block because of the uncertainties in the world today – including our continued war or terror?

Far Left: Cut the military we do not need as much of it as we have.

Far Right: Do not cut a dime. We need it all. In fact, spend more.

From the Middle: Modest cuts must be made. It is fiscal insanity to think otherwise. The military needs to spend more wisely – on special operation forces rather than conventional forces, on the air force and navy rather than the infantry. We must not lose sight of the fact that it is our military power that helps maintain our position as *the* world power – both militarily and economically. Why do you think the world's reserve currency is the United States dollar? It is because if anything goes wrong in the world, the world knows that America's military will protect America and the rest of the free world. It would be an interesting study to determine how much of the dollar's value would be lost if we allowed our military to lose its world-power stature.

49. China (America's new archrival)

Definition: Are they stealing our secrets? What are their territorial intentions? Do they manipulate their currency so we keep buying cheap stuff from them? Why do they lend us so much money? Will they overtake us as the world's economic and military power? This is another scary one.

Far Left: There is nothing to worry about.

Far Right: China plans on global domination.

<u>From the Middle</u>: We borrow way too much money from China just so we can purchase those inexpensive products they make (the same products that shut down our factories). China is a potential military threat, and they have manipulated their currency. We need to invest in a lot of diplomacy in China, maintain our strong military, and become more economically competitive to keep China at bay. It will take a minimum of ten years (and probably much longer) for the Chinese to catch us militarily. However, China can overtake us as the world's largest economy within ten years - if we do not get our economic situation under control. We will be hard pressed to fend off whatever global ambitions China may have if we allow them to overtake us as the world's economic power. The Cold War with Russia was won on the economic playing field, <u>NOT</u> the military battleground. Hopefully, our diplomatic efforts will result in a friendly China with a more open society. By the way, there is much social unrest in China. Its people desperately want the freedoms that we enjoy. Unfortunately, the Chinese government is very efficient at censoring the internet and squashing any uprisings before they can gather any critical mass. The Chinese know how to prevent an "Arab Spring". In China, as in all parts of the world, a more open society would mean a more rational and a more friendly government. The Chinese will not be able to suppress the masses forever – not in this age of technology enabled communications. Likewise, we cannot forever fend off the Chinese from overtaking us as the world's largest economy. They have a population of 1.3 billion people. However, the longer we can fend China off, the more likely it will be for them to have an open society once they do surpass us.

50. North Korea

Definition: North Korea has nuclear weapons but does not have any long range missiles to threaten the United States (yet). They are a rogue nation that has starved its population of food and information. With the recent death of their supreme leader, the supreme leader's twenty-nine year old son is now in charge.   He is inexperienced, immature, and probably believes he has to prove himself to be a tough guy.

Far Left: Negotiate with them. They need food aid and will make concessions on their rocket development for food.

Far Right: No more negotiations. They have reneged on so many past negotiations that to attempt any new deal would be foolish.

From the Middle: Continue the current path of multi-lateral negotiations with China, South Korea, Russia, Japan and the United States. This is a scary issue but is there anything that we can accomplish here? This is another reason to spend a lot of money on diplomacy with China.

51. The United Nations

Definition: The United Nations is ineffective in bringing rogue nations in line because Russia and China are permanent members of the Security Council. As such, they have veto power over any resolution. Should the United States continue to be the largest funder of the United Nations? Should we give up on the UN altogether? Should we just focus our international policy making with our NATO partners?

Far Left: No changes to the United States funding or participation in the United Nations. It is the only place available for world dialogue.

<u>Far Right</u>: Quit the United Nations and work with our NATO partners on global policy matters. China and Russia have tied our hands for far too long. Why waste more time and money?

<u>From the Middle</u>: Maintain our funding and participation in the United Nations. However, when Russia and/or China tie our hands, we should then work with our NATO partners (which now includes Turkey) to establish needed regional policies. This will allow us to provide the dignity of human rights to people that are now denied such fundamental rights because of the United Nations' ineffectiveness. Did you know that there are now twenty-eight members of NATO? Non-members of NATO that we should also include in our collaborations include (but are not limited to): Australia, Japan, Mexico, and New Zealand.

There are always new issues on the horizon. November is six months away from when the above list was developed. Somebody will dig up some dirt on somebody. A new issue will be born. Or, the world will change with another Arab Spring, natural disaster, or conflict somewhere on the planet. The list above will never be complete, but it does paint the general picture of the current issues.

So, with so many issues how are you to decide who to elect for president, senator, or congressman?

3. THE GRABBER

There are so many issues because there are 330 million Americans. That long list of issues may have one that is _THE_ issue for you. It may be the only thing that matters to you. If a candidate takes your position on that issue but does not take your position on every other matter – you will still vote for him or her. This is not unreasonable. Think of the gay person that has been unofficially married for decades and is now nearing end of life. He or she desperately wants their life partner to have all the privileges that straight married couples have. It is not hard to understand that gay and lesbian rights are the _ONLY_ issue that matters to this person.

Now consider the illegal immigrant with a handful of children living in the United States. Mom desperately wants her children to be able to go to school and get an education. But, she is also afraid that by doing so, the whole family could be identified for deportation. It is not hard to understand that immigration is the _ONLY_ issue that matters to her. She might not be able to vote, but she probably has some family member that can.

More than one billion dollars will be spent on the presidential election campaign alone. If we added up the senatorial and congressional campaign spending; who knows how much will be spent? One billion dollars is equal to $3 for every man, woman and child in the United States. Considering that only a third of every man, woman and child will vote – it is about $10 a vote.

If you are a one-issue voter – it is understandable. Just try to consider that statesmanship and leadership are important factors too.

4. THE ECONOMY

You may have one of those "grabber" issues that will make your voting decisions easy. However, for the majority of Americans, the most pressing issue is the economy. The economy includes; the national debt, taxes, energy, Social Security, Medicare, the Affordable Care Act, Afghanistan, the military, the environment – and, of course: jobs, jobs, jobs.

In 2008 our national debt was $10 trillion. At the end of April, 2012, it was $15.6 trillion. In less than four years, our federal government has spent $5.6 trillion dollars more than the taxes it collected. The United States Gross Domestic Product ("GDP" - a measure of all goods and services bought and sold) will be approximately $15 trillion this year. We owe more than we produce in a full year!

However, this does not mean that we have to turn off the federal spending machine today. In fact, the accelerated spending of the past few years was necessary to heal the ailing economy. When a patient shows up at the emergency room with an open wound and lung cancer – you treat the open wound first and the cancer second.

Well Congress is good at open wounds. Congress is not good at the long-term stuff. Congress can pass a $787 billion spending stimulus package to help stop the bleeding in a matter of days. Congress cannot stop the spending to treat the cancer for years.

Signs of economic improvement can be found everywhere. Unemployment is slowly coming down. Economic growth keeps reporting on the plus side - quarter after quarter. The American economy is mending. However, at the end of 2012 all the Bush tax cuts are due to expire. The Social Security payroll tax holiday is also due to expire. Will this reduction in extra pocket change slow the economy down? Of course it will. But, it should not slow it so much that we see the feared double-dip recession. Besides, Congress will not allow the Bush tax cuts to expire for the middle class (anyone making less than $500K or $1 million). The plan is to slowly back out the government stimulus and allow the private sector to grow on its own. The kick start that was needed has been given – now it is up to us to keep it going.

One cautionary note: the economy is improving. However, it is mostly a corporate recovery. American companies are practicing capitalism - as they should. That means they are manufacturing goods in places of the world where cheap labor is available (e.g.: China, Mexico) and selling it where the consumers live – America. We may see the unemployment curve tick up and back down again before we fully ride out the Great Recession. We may even see a quarter or two with economic contraction (negative growth). Europe's problems will affect us as well – hopefully not too much. Hold on to your hat, we are in for a bumpy ride – but the overall trend is in the right direction. Now that you have been warned, let's get back to our government spending.

Even with the end of the "stimulus", government spending is not being cut enough. There is not even a plan for cutting enough spending and/or raising revenue so that we actually spend within the limits of our income (the collected taxes). This is the long-term stuff that Congress cannot do. While our national debt was $15.6 trillion at the end of April, 2012 – it will be $16.4 trillion by the end of 2012 – and, still growing.

Our gross domestic product of $15 trillion is the equivalent of the entire economy "earning" $15 trillion. It is the "earnings" of every man, woman, and child of the United States. The government is only getting some percentage of that in taxes. In fact, the federal government collects approximately $2.5 trillion per year in taxes. The government "earns" about $2.5 trillion per year and owes $15.6 trillion. But that is not the real problem. The real problem is that the government continues to spend more than it collects in taxes – approximately $1.2 trillion more each year. The non-partisan Congressional Budget Office projects that our national debt will continue to grow indefinitely due to the spending commitments already in place. We are on the path to PIGdom! (Portugal, Italy, Ireland, Greece and Spain are called the PIGS because of their unbearably high public debt to GDP ratio). This is true insanity.

Unfortunately, this is a slow building problem (although it has accelerated in the past few years). The catastrophe will not hit us until after the next election cycle so Congress will not do anything about it. It may not threaten to cripple the economy until after the 2016 election campaign – so Congress will not do anything until after 2016. Then, the federal government will owe so much money that it will have to borrow every dollar available in the marketplace - making it impossible for businesses to borrow – limiting businesses ability to grow - and causing interest rates to soar. The government will not be able to afford anything but the interest payments on the debt. No more Social Security, no more Medicare, no more military, no more food stamps. The riots you see on the news in Athens – they will be happening in New York, Philadelphia, Chicago, Atlanta, Los Angeles and almost everywhere in the United States.

Some may call this "fear mongering" and it is a little exaggerated. The riots may not occur until 2020.

Compounding this government spending addiction is the new global economy. We are losing jobs to Brazil, Russia, India, China and others (the BRICs). Recently there was a news story carried by all the national broadcast television companies regarding Apple. The story stated that the Chinese factory workers making all of our iPads, iPhones, and iPods were working in horrible conditions. They routinely work 80 or more hours per week and only get paid $700 per month. The Chinese are getting paid about $2 per hour with no premium for overtime. If they do get paid time-and-a-half for overtime, their wages are $1.63 per hour. Similarly, The New York Times had a story a few months ago reporting that Mexican factories are now making all the electronic circuit boards for American car manufacturers. The Mexicans sitting at a workbench get paid about $15 per day – or close to the Chinese' $2 per hour. When President Obama met with Steve Jobs and asked how America could get those jobs back – Steve Jobs told the president "Mr. President, those jobs are never coming back".

Our government spends more than the revenue it takes in - and year after year adds to our national debt. In a similar manner, we as American consumers purchase more foreign goods than we sell back to the rest of the world. Anybody see a trend here? How long can we keep doing this? We love our cheap, big-screen TVs. But what happens if China asks us to give back the $2 trillion they lent us? The printing presses will start spinning and the value of the dollar will shrink overnight. Those big-screen TVs will not be cheap anymore because it will take a lot more of those freshly printed dollars to purchase one. This may be the inevitable end-game. Inflation will also artificially raise the gross domestic product and thereby make our debt a smaller percentage of GDP.

Should it even be mentioned that we import more than one-fifth of our energy when we have the natural resources right under our feet? Let's just keep giving our money and our jobs away. The main reason we do this is not because we do not have the energy. It is because the environmentalist do not want us to drill, dig, or "frac" for it ("frac" is short for the hydraulic fracturing process used to extract natural gas from rock). They also do not want us to burn coal. Most of our current coal burning plants are dirty – but clean coal technologies are available – and we must use them. Oil on the other hand is non-defensible. We cannot drill for oil because we might have a spill? We cannot build a pipeline to bring oil from Canada? But it is okay for other nations to drill for the oil, pipe it over their land to a sea port, load it onto tankers and ship it half way around the world to us? What if that other country has a spill? Don't we care? Who do you trust more to protect the environment, a company under the watchful eyes of the United States government or China drilling off the shore of Cuba? Is the environment not a global concern?

To fix our economy, we need smaller government through spending cuts, economic growth that will create a broader tax base, higher tax rates to pay off our debt, and a sound energy policy that is not held hostage by the environmentalists. Later these principles will be discussed in "Fixing the Economy". Before we get to that discussion, the need for compassion and statesmanship in America will be discussed.

5. POVERTY IN AMERICA

The following information has been copied from the United States Census Bureau's website. Not all of the information in the related announcement is included and some of the paragraphs have been reordered. You can visit the Census Bureau's website and view the entire announcement in its original form. This information is included here because while those fortunate among us are demanding spending cuts, we must not lose sight of the facts. The economic conditions have caused great hardships. The Great Society of President Johnson did wonderful things to help alleviate poverty in America. We must continue our compassion. Hopefully, this information will put this book's demand for sensible fiscal policy in perspective: fiscal sensibility, but continued compassion. This information loudly broadcasts that the Tea Party must recognize that compromise is the only way forward.

"The U.S. Census Bureau announced today (September 13, 2011) that in 2010, median household income declined, the poverty rate increased and the

percentage without health insurance coverage was not statistically different from the previous year.

Real median household income in the United States in 2010 was $49,445, a 2.3 percent decline from the 2009 median.

The nation's official poverty rate in 2010 was 15.1 percent, up from 14.3 percent in 2009 — the third consecutive annual increase in the poverty rate. There were 46.2 million people in poverty in 2010, up from 43.6 million in 2009 — the fourth consecutive annual increase and the largest number in the 52 years for which poverty estimates have been published.

The number of people without health insurance coverage rose from 49.0 million in 2009 to 49.9 million in 2010, while the percentage without coverage −16.3 percent - was not statistically different from the rate in 2009.

This information covers the first full calendar year after the December 2007-June 2009 recession. See section on the historical impact of recessions.

These findings are contained in the report <u>Income, Poverty, and Health Insurance Coverage in the United States: 2010</u>. The following results for the nation were compiled from information collected in the 2011 Current Population Survey (CPS) Annual Social and Economic Supplement (ASEC):

Thresholds

> • *As defined by the Office of Management and Budget and updated for inflation using the Consumer Price Index, the weighted average poverty threshold*

for a family of four in 2010 was $22,314.

Poverty

• *The poverty rate in 2010 was the highest since 1993 but was 7.3 percentage points lower than the poverty rate in 1959, the first year for which poverty estimates are available. Since 2007, the poverty rate has increased by 2.6 percentage points.*

• *In 2010, the family poverty rate and the number of families in poverty were 11.7 percent and 9.2 million, respectively, up from 11.1 percent and 8.8 million in 2009.*

• *The poverty rate and the number in poverty increased for both married-couple families (6.2 percent and 3.6 million in 2010 from 5.8 percent and 3.4 million in 2009) and female-householder-with-no-husband-present families (31.6 percent and 4.7 million in 2010 from 29.9 percent and 4.4 million in 2009). For families with a male householder no wife present, the poverty rate and the number in poverty were not statistically different from 2009 (15.8 percent and 880,000 in 2010).*

Age

• *The poverty rate increased for children younger than 18 (from 20.7 percent in 2009 to 22.0 percent in 2010) and people 18 to 64 (from 12.9 percent in 2009 to 13.7 percent in 2010), while it was not statistically different for people 65 and older (9.0 percent).*

• *Similar to the patterns observed for the poverty rate in 2010, the number of people in poverty increased for children younger than 18 (15.5 million in 2009 to 15.6 million in 2010) and people 18 to 64 (24.7 million in 2009 to 26.3 million in 2010) and was not statistically different for people 65 and older (3.5 million).*

Health Insurance Coverage

• *The number of people with health insurance increased to 256.2 million in 2010 from 255.3 million in 2009. The percentage of people with health insurance was not statistically different from 2009.*

• *Between 2009 and 2010, the percentage of people covered by private health insurance declined from 64.5 percent to 64.0 percent, while the percentage covered by government health insurance increased from 30.6 percent to 31.0 percent. The percentage covered by employment-based health insurance declined from 56.1 percent to 55.3 percent.*

• *The percentage covered by Medicaid (15.9 percent) was not statistically different from 2009.*

• *In 2010, 9.8 percent of children under 18 (7.3 million) were without health insurance. Neither estimate is significantly different from the corresponding 2009 estimate.*

• *The uninsured rate for children in poverty (15.4 percent) was greater than the rate for all children (9.8 percent).*

• *In 2010, the uninsured rates decreased as household income increased from 26.9 percent for those in households with annual incomes less than $25,000 to 8.0 percent in households with incomes of $75,000 or more.*

Income

   • Since 2007, the year before the most recent recession, real median household income has declined 6.4 percent and is 7.1 percent below the median household income peak that occurred prior to the 2001 recession in 1999. The percentages are not statistically different from each another.

Earnings

   • In 2010, the earnings of women who worked full time, year-round were 77 percent of that for men working full time, year-round, not statistically different from the 2009 ratio. The 2010 real median earnings of these men and women were not different from the 2009 earnings.

   • Since 2007, the number of men working full time, year-round with earnings decreased by 6.6 million and the number of corresponding women declined by 2.8 million.

Historical Impact of Recessions

Since 2010 represents the first full calendar year after the recession that ended in June 2009, one can compare changes in income, poverty and health insurance coverage between 2009 and 2010 with changes during the first year after the end of other recessions:

   • Median household income declined the first full year following the December 2007 to June 2009 recession, as well as in the first full year following three other recessions (March 2001 to November 2001, January 1980 to July 1980 and December 1969 to November 1970). However, household *income increased the first full year following the November 1973 to March 1975 recession, and the changes following the July 1990 to March 1991 and July 1981 to November 1982 recessions were not statistically significant.*

• The poverty rate and the number of people in poverty increased in the first calendar year following the end of the last three recessions. For the recessions that ended in 1961 and 1975, the poverty rate decreased in the next full calendar year.

• After the most recent recession, there was no significant difference in the uninsured rate during the first full year after the recession. However, in the year following the recessions that ended in 1991 and 2001, the uninsured rate increased."

6. THE POLITICS

Political science is taught in schools as the methods for developing public policy that reflects society's values and needs. Politics as practiced in America is about creating a contrast between one candidate and another; so that the voter can make a clear choice of who he or she wants to elect. The Far Left and the Far Right establish position statements on every issue imaginable just to create that contrast. If you are a Republican you better adhere to the positions of the Far Right (at least during primary season). Democrats must adhere to the positions of the Far Left (again, at least during primary season). Unfortunately, even after the general elections, the forces of Washington require the office holder to execute his or her office according to their party's orthodoxy. This has created political self-righteousness.

This political self-righteousness is due to a lack of leadership, and a lack of statesmen. It is also because we as Americans have become too polarized. Half of us are watching MSNBC and enjoying the Far Left bash the Far Right. The other half is watching Fox News and enjoying the Far Right bash the Far Left. The news media has made politics not just a spectator sport but a participant sport – call in to your favorite talk show and bash away. It has ingrained a vitriol atmosphere of mistrust of anyone that is not on "your side". That is not the America that our founding fathers created – and if we do not fix it, America will lose its place as the shining city on a hill. (To be fair, it must be stated that Fox News is no where near as one-sided as MSNBC. In fact, NBC has created a monster that threatens its own legitimacy as a serious news agency.)

The way Washington works these days, you are voting for a party not a person. Washington has been deranged by the 24-hour news cycle. There are so many TV news channels, newspapers, magazines and blogs that a politician cannot take a ten minute walk without some reporter quizzing him about his position on some random issue. If the politician does not give the designated party response, he or she makes the evening news as a rebel. Soon thereafter the party leaders take him or her out behind the wood shed for a little attitude correction.

Remember the days when politics was not covered like an entertainment gossip show? Back in those days, politicians could privately debate the other side and actually partake in a little give and take. It is a shame that the days of statesmanship in Washington are gone.

In the summer of 2011, Congress had to raise the debt limit for the United States of America. This has been routinely done many times in the past. The question of whether or not to raise the debt limit has never been used for political purposes. But in the summer of 2011, the Tea Party decided to draw a line in the sand. They announced that there would be no approval of a higher debt limit if there was not a commitment to spending cuts to bring the debt under control. This was the peak of our political gridlock. We have been stuck at this low point ever since. (It is a shame that there is no humor in the "peak" being our low point.)

Back in 2011, President Obama and Speaker Boehner played a round of golf together. Afterward, they announced that they may have reached an enormous breakthrough on the debt/budget crisis. It was a deal that would cut $4 trillion off the national debt in the next ten years. Speaker Boehner then went back to his Republican caucus and was told: NO NEW TAXES. The deal that could have cut $4 trillion dollars off the national debt fell apart. Soon thereafter, the United States of America's debt rating was lowered. Partisan politics derailed what could have been a great accomplishment for America. It did not happen, and we are still staring down the barrel of the gun – that of becoming the next PIG.

Had Ronald Reagan been president and Tip O'Neill been the Speaker, we probably would have seen that big deal. We would be better off today. We really need statesmen. If you find statesmen, no matter what party affiliation they have - vote for them. They do not adhere to the strict Far Left/Far Right rules. They lead the ideological self-righteous politicians to where America needs to go.

Speaking of ideological self-righteousness: The Tea Party started with a wave of enthusiasm that hit a nerve with Americans. They spoke of fiscal responsibility when most Americans were just becoming aware of our fiscal mess. They raised the awareness of a very important issue that did not appear be on Washington's agenda. They gained popularity – then they became full of themselves and thought they could do no wrong. They became the embodiment of ideological self-righteousness. Once you hit that line of becoming an ideological self-righteous anything – you cannot compromise. When you cannot compromise, you cannot get anything done in politics. Will some leader from the Tea Party please stand up and demonstrate some statesmanship? Yes, we Americans want fiscal sanity. But that does not mean that we are willing to throw the downtrodden under the bus. We have to cut spending but we have to raise taxes too.

The foolish manner in which Congress passed the Affordable Care Act bill led many Americans to mistrust their own government. It was the trigger that transformed the Tea Party from a group wanting to reform Washington, to a group intent on shutting Washington down. The Senate has rules for passing bills. A bill as significant as the Affordable Care Act bill should not have been passed through a budgeting, loop-hole provision called "reconciliation". The reason that sixty members of the senate are required to bring a bill to a vote is to assure that the law is sound public policy – policy that reflects society's values and needs. Without the sixty senators, a filibuster can delay the vote from ever taking place. The manner in which the Affordable Care Act was passed heightened the unwillingness of the Republicans to work with the Democrats (even though the Republicans have used the same trick in the past). Being unwilling to work with the Democrats _was_ understandable. However, it is no longer understandable. We have big problems to fix. Both sides must work together as soon as possible.

It was not included in the list of issues – but the lack of statesmen is the biggest issue facing America today. The second biggest issue is the "big-money" corruption of our political process.

7. THE STATESMAN (gender neutral)

It is not just the president. We need leaders at every level of policy making that can change the way we do business. We need leaders to replace Senators Evan Bayh of Indiana, Olympia Snowe of Maine, and Joseph Lieberman of Connecticut. These three Senators (a Democrat, a Republican, and an Independent) are precisely the leaders we need. They have practiced the art of politics. They have shined the light of the American ideals, and they have compromised and communicated. Now, frustrated with the current political gridlock, all are leaving (Senator Bayh actually left in 2010). They do not like the new American political sport. Their departure, and their reasons for departing, should tell us something about ourselves. We have gone too far.

We need more leaders like good old Congressman Thomas "Tip" O'Neill, from Massachusetts. Without the Democratic Tip, Republican President Reagan could not have accomplished anything. Everyone remembers President Reagan as a great president. Very few people remember that Speaker Tip O'Neill was the willing statesman that worked with President Reagan to get things done.

President Clinton was a statesman. He had to deal with Speaker Gingrich. To hear Speaker Gingrich's story you would think that he worked cooperatively with President Clinton to enact legislation that spurred economic growth and reformed welfare. Others' recollection of the time was that Speaker Gingrich held a gun to President Clinton's head and President Clinton was the statesman that conceded enough to get some of what he believed the country needed.

Senators Scott Brown of Massachusetts and Bob Casey, Jr. of Pennsylvania may be statesmen. They have not been around long enough to truly judge. But, they have not always voted along party lines. When you see campaign advertisements that claim a candidate has a 99% voting record as a true conservative or a true liberal – kick them out. The world is not that black and white. If a candidate has that kind of a track record can you really expect them to compromise on the big deal that is needed to solve America's ever growing debt problem. Somebody has to raise their hand and say "Yes, I'll give $1 dollar of tax increases for every $10 dollars of spending cuts". Or any other proportion of taxes versus spending cuts – because we need both! And, that takes courage.

Courage is another trait of statesmen. Congressman Ryan has demonstrated courage by writing a budget bill that seeks to remedy our nation's economic problems. He communicates very well, and if he is willing to negotiate the points of his budget bill (including raising taxes) – he will demonstrate all the qualities of a statesman. Congressman Ryan may be one of the people that shines the light of the American ideals – and leads the way to the riddance of ideological self-righteousness. We will see.

Individual Americans must stop being political sport spectators that vehemently cheer our team while denouncing the other team. We are all Americans. We have to change our collective behavior so that the statesmen can return. All you media executives out there – this means you too! Why can't we have civilized discourse? Does it not sell enough newspapers or TV commercials?

Our founding fathers were statesmen. They built a nation by combining thirteen individual nations. They had many differences and they argued them vehemently. In the end, they gave up their own sovereignty, compromised and formed a more perfect union. However, there was one issue that they could not solve – slavery. Those statesmen decided to put it off for a latter day. In fact, they agreed that it would not be addressed until at least 1808. They never got around to dealing with it – and the Civil War was the result. Let's learn from history and deal with this huge issue of our economy.

If we are to ever correct the issue of "Money Corrupting the Political Process" we must have statesmanship. We must find leaders that can develop public policy for the American populace – _NOT_ the special-interest groups. A statesman that can gather so much populace support because of his or her charisma and statesmanship will stop the special-interest groups from dictating our public policy. Once there is one such individual, more will follow.

8. FIXING THE ECONOMY

Only 50% of Americans currently pay federal income taxes. Worse still, almost 50% of Americans receive some government assistance. We cannot sustain this entitlement state. It will bankrupt us. The European austerity programs have no merit – have you seen the riots in Athens? There are only two ways out of a national debt crisis – strong economic growth that austerity by its very nature precludes, or through hyper inflation. Obviously hyper inflation is not a pain free remedy. In the United States, we are experiencing economic growth. It is weak growth, but it is growth nonetheless. By staggering in the expiration of the Bush tax cuts, we can sustain our growth while demonstrating a commitment to the bond markets that we are serious about addressing our national debt. This will allow us to maintain interest rates at the current historical lows.

Let the Bush tax cuts expire at the end of 2012 for anyone earning $500K or more, at the end of 2013 for anyone earning $200K or more, and for all Americans at the end of 2014. *The middle class of America must pay some federal income taxes or this will no longer be*

America. Hard working people need to contribute to society when they can – and our middle class can and wants to contribute. They want to be a part of making and keeping America great. To think that just raising the taxes on the wealthiest of Americans will solve our problems is ridiculous. We must broaden our tax base if we are to seriously attack our fiscal problems.

If we do not demonstrate to the bond markets that we are serious about addressing our national debt, our debt rating will be lowered again. A lower rating means we pay higher interest on our debt. We will face the downward spiral of a growing debt, slowing economic activity, and another recession – an even bigger one!

People must pay more taxes but we must *STOP* taxing businesses. Everyone knows that when you tax a business, the business has to include that tax in the price of the goods and/or services that it sells. So the taxes are really paid for by the people buying the products. But, when that buyer is not an American, we are putting ourselves at a disadvantage. In a globally competitive economy, should we be adding taxes to the price of goods and services we want to sell to foreign countries?

The argument that raising personal income taxes is the same as raising small business taxes has very little merit. Yes, there are many small business owners that are sole proprietors. These are the *very* small businesses. Once an individual has grown a business to a size that is sufficient to employ tens of people, he or she incorporates the business. A successful businessperson knows that the corporate organization protects his or her personal wealth from lawsuits against their business. So the call here to eliminate business taxes is directed at corporate income taxes and all excise taxes that impact our exports.

Another area that must be addressed is energy. Drill Baby Drill! Frac Baby Frac! Lease all the government land we have for drilling and require that the oil drilled on government land to be refined in America and sold to Americans at a fair price (cost plus a reasonable profit). Invest in clean coal technologies so we can use more of America's most abundant source of energy. We have enough energy – it should be inexpensive for Americans – and for American businesses. That will reduce the cost of producing our products – and give us a trade advantage. We should be able to export energy!

The last area that we must attack is health care. America's health care costs are higher than the rest of the world. That cost is embedded in the prices of the products we sell to the rest of the world. Therefore, our high health care costs make us less competitive in the global economy. The Affordable Care Act did not reduce the cost of health care – it *increased* the cost. It is great that our children can stay on our company provided health care plans until they are twenty-six. It is also great that no one can be denied health care for pre-existing conditions. However, these changes have increased the cost of health care.

It will take us longer than it should, but we will eventually get to a single-payer, socialized health care system. Beginning in 2014, businesses that do not provide health care benefits will either have to start providing health care benefits or be fined. The established fine is eight percent of the business's payroll. This fine will start the process to socialized health care. The fine is less than the cost of health care benefits. Therefore, businesses will elect to pay the eight percent fine. Even companies that provide health care benefits today will stop doing so - to save money. The majority of workers will be placed on the government sponsored health care plan. Over time, all Americans will be on the government sponsored plan. Only then, will our health care costs be reduced – thereby making us more globally competitive. The Affordable Care Act is flawed. We should move to a single-payer, socialized health care system today. Those more fortunate among us will be able to purchase "add-on coverage" and continue to enjoy the high level of health care that they now receive. One final word on the Affordable Care Act – once we actually have socialized health care, people should pay for it – *NOT* businesses. A flat-rate payroll tax (of say 8%) should be charged to employees *NOT* employers. We do not want more taxes embedded in the products we are trying to sell to the rest of the world.

Lower energy costs, lower health care costs and less of a tax burden on businesses will make America more competitive. So now that we have established a basis for competing in the global economy - what are we going to make? Textiles and electronics are gone. All the manufacturing jobs that do not require large capital investments are gone. Or, they are on their way out the door. You do not have to invest large sums of money to have someone sit at a workbench and solder electronic parts together. Similarly, sewing machines do not require large sums of money to purchase. That is why textile and electronic manufacturing have gone so quickly. They are inexpensive businesses to start. And, when the labor costs are only $2 per hour, where would you place your workbench or sewing machine? On the other hand, building large equipment (i.e.: automobiles, trains, airplanes, bulldozers, power plant turbines, etc.) requires a large capital investment. So even if you can hire auto workers for $2 an hour in China and Mexico, would you want to risk building a billion dollar plant in China or Mexico? The laws of property protection are an advantage of the United States.

Big equipment manufacturing is where America has to focus. It means more big business and less small business (in the manufacturing sector). It means more automation so that less manpower is required – but that is exactly how we are going to compete. Large equipment costs a lot of money to ship across the world so we have to automate as much as possible and build these products as cost effectively as possible. This means that tax incentives for manufacturing investment are a must. It also means we must not allow our government debt burden to result in a lack of money being available to invest in new factories – or to not be available at reasonable interest rates.

Since the call for eliminating all business taxes has already been sounded in this book, we must be creative in developing our incentives for investments in American factories. An easy choice would be to eliminate or reduce the capital gains tax on personal income. The same could be done for dividends paid by American companies. Other incentives could include loan guarantees to _PROVEN_ businesses that manufacture in America ("proven" meaning not the Solyndras of the world).

Cisco is currently running a television commercial where they show a completely automated factory. It appears as though the robotic arms are placing car door pieces in place while another robotic arm reaches in and welds the pieces together. Another robotic arm picks the welded assembly up and moves it to the next station of the manufacturing process. There are tens of these robotic arms humming along without a human in sight. Then all of a sudden, one of the robotic arms emits a puff of smoke and starts to blink a sign of trouble. After the one robot fails, the whole assembly line shuts down. Just then, another robotic arm reaches in and fixes the broken robot and the assembly line starts humming again. A human being is never seen. This is what our manufacturing is becoming: fewer jobs, but the ability to sell in a global market. Obviously, the Cisco commercial is not reality and there will always be the need for some humans to supervise the robots, but it will be fewer and fewer.

Human beings will still develop the ideas of what to build, and design the manufacturing machines - like the robotic factory. These new factories should be treated like military secrets. Unfortunately, they will not. These robots will be sold to any country that has the money to buy them. We will export the machines that put our workers out of business and then put our robots out of business. This is what capitalism is all about. In the long run it will benefit us – even if we do experience some pain and suffering in the interim.

Maybe we should provide employers that treat their robots like military secrets the tax break of not having to pay the employers' share of the social security and Medicare taxes (assuming that we have already stopped taxing them on all business profits).

Hopefully, some young engineer is already designing electronic parts (capacitors, resisters, inductors, etc.) that can either be soldered by a robot or plugged into a board (rather than soldering) by a robot. Of course the robot needs to be designed too. Maybe our research and development investments will replace these electronic parts with some type of "block" – just like the microprocessor "chip" replaced our vacuum tubes and transistors. Then we can get those jobs back that Apple's Steve Jobs told the president were never coming back.

Our jobs will be in engineering new products and the robots to make them. There will always be a need for farmers, accountants, marketing people, lawyers, computer science engineers (to develop our video games and the new facebooks); tradesmen (because we will continue to build and repair our own homes), energy workers of all kinds, and workers in the services sector (travel, dining, entertainment, building and home maintenance, and cleaning up after ourselves). The service sector of our economy will be where small business has the advantage over big business.

The above list of jobs is not intended to be complete – just a listing of what the majority of our jobs will be in the future. Guess what, they are not that much different than they are right now.

We have been moving to more of a service economy for years. Our robots will push us more quickly into a service economy. That is why we need the best robots (and why they should be treated like military secrets). So, we can have cost effective products to sell to the rest of the world. We cannot afford to just provide services to each other and purchase all our products from other countries. That, like our national debt, is fiscal insanity.

The vast size of the available workforce in the emerging markets (1.3 billion people in China alone) means that labor costs will not rise above the $2 per hour threshold for decades. Once the world has reached full employment (in the developed sense of commerce); labor rates will begin to rise. Until that happens we will be fighting an uphill battle. Our standard of living will not continue to rise as it has since the start of our nation. We will stagnate (maybe even lower our standard of living) as the emerging markets rise to our level. Then, once that breakeven point has been reached – we too (along with the rest of the developed world) will start to see our standard of living rise. Once the emerging markets actually emerge, the market will be enormous with more consumers than ever. Trade will flourish with the benefits of all people becoming wealthier.

Until the emerging markets actually emerge we are looking at a dismal picture. But it is the picture we see when looking through the telescope – with today's political gridlock. Is there anything we can do to make it better? Yes, but it requires statesmanship to develop sound public policy based on leveraging our strengths.

The strengths the United States has are: an entrepreneurial spirit, imagination, research and development, a risk taking financial system, a talented work force, a strong education system, the infrastructure of roads, railways, ports, and the internet - and the rule of law. We also have vast natural resources. Above all, we are the largest consumer market in the world. It does not cost us anything to ship to ourselves (well at least not the cost of shipping across a sea).

We do have one weakness – political gridlock. Actually our weakness is in our collective divisive behavior that political sport has riled up in us. We must remain passionate, but we must be more rational. We must eliminate all of our "no-compromise" positions. This does not mean that we have to eliminate our principles. It just means that we have to be willing to compromise. How else can we establish public policy that reduces our health care costs, reduces our energy costs, shifts our tax burden from businesses to people, provides incentives to invest in automated factories, and reduces our national debt?

Once we have made those public policy changes we need to consider one more fundamental change – the length of our workweek.

We have already automated so much that we have squeezed our employment to the point where 8% may be the new norm. Do you remember when a businessperson wrote a letter by hand? Then he or she gave it to his or her secretary who typed it – and used "white out" to correct any errors. Who has a secretary type for them anymore? The US Postal Service has been almost automated off the face of the earth with email. The sets of televisions studios no longer have humans behind the cameras. Instead of six cameramen and a director, there are now six robotic cameras being manipulated by one person at a control panel. And, although the Cisco TV commercial is a little futuristic, our factories have been automated to reduce the amount of labor to build things. To remain competitive, we must automate more.

We have to realize that all of our automation has impacted our employment. It is time to start thinking about a shorter work week. A shorter work week would mean more time for leisure and more consumption of entertainment – another American strength. We are the largest consumer market on the planet. We need to do more to buy American products and entertainment is a great place to start.

We are also the bread basket of the world. Reducing taxes and the health care and energy costs embedded in our food exports will allow us to export even more food.

Another strength is our military. It is because of our military strength that the United States dollar is the reserve currency of the world. The Chinese are comfortable in lending us $2 trillion because of our military. Our military maintains the strength of our dollar higher than it would be if market forces were the sole determinant of its value. Selling military products to worthy nations is also good for our balance of trade.

Maybe the Chinese are willing to lend us so much money because they realize that they can pull the string on us and cripple our ability to continue spending so much on our military. That is a scary thought – but one that we should consider in our strategic planning.

We have so many strengths that we cannot allow our political weakness to bring us down. We need statesmen that understand the economy. The statesmen will, by their nature, consider the human side of the economy. They will develop appropriate entitlement reform; reform that will necessarily cut costs but will not create undo hardship for the most unfortunate among us.

We cannot compete with the $2 per hour labor in the emerging markets. But, the emerging markets do not have what we have – the infrastructure, inexpensive energy, capital to invest, automation know-how, research and development and the largest consumer market in the world. We will not compete with $2 per hour labor – but we will be competitive.

9. AMERICA'S FUTURE

Americans will learn how to live in the twenty-four by seven news cycle, the world of constant political talk radio, ideological television shows, the world of the blogosphere and the world of Twitter. We will remain passionate but also realize that people are not bad because of their political party affiliation. _We will realize that ideological self-righteousness is wrong_. One person will emerge with the message of this book and win a campaign because of it. People will take notice of this courageous person and will listen to him or her. Then we will see other leaders come forward. We as a people will evolve.

The statesman will enact legislation that rids our system of big-money corruption. This legislation will return America to its citizens (as opposed to the special-interest groups). Once this occurs, people will hearken back to the words of President Kennedy and believe in them again: "Ask not what your country can do for you – ask what you can do for your country".

People will believe in their government again. Then, we as a people will start acting as rational, reasonable human beings. More and more statesmen will return. Maybe even Senators Bayh, Snowe, and Lieberman will return. Well probably not these Senators, but people like them will return. We will still be passionate, but we will not be self-righteous. We will consider others' opinions. Then, we will value others' opinions.

A new era of statesmanship in America will bring about less spending, higher personal income taxes, less business taxes, continued compassion – and increased prosperity. The increased prosperity will broaden the tax base and after time, will allow for taxes to be cut. In the interim, we must pay for the sins of our past.

Finding the first statesman is _NOT_ the hard part. He or she will come forward. The hard part is for all Americans to allow statesmanship – or at least a majority of Americans. Less divisive behavior by the collective masses will result in more statesmanship in Washington.

"Tweet" to all Americans: "We Democrats, we Republicans, and we Independents are _ALL_ in this together – let's keep America great _together_. Let us _compromise_."

And that is the view from Fairway Frank; the little guy looking upward from the middle of the road.

ABOUT THE AUTHOR

I was raised in a blue-collar, hard working, lower-middle class neighborhood of West Philadelphia. It was the same neighborhood that the Fresh Prince of Bel Air (Will Smith) left for safety reasons. In fact, Will Smith went to the same grade school that I attended. I even coached him in CYO (Catholic Youth Organization) football. I can view the world from many angles because of my austere upbringing and the many life successes with which I have been blessed.

I had very humble beginnings but America gave me the opportunity to become an engineer, a management consultant, a corporate vice-president, a small business owner – and now, an author. However, it was not until I reached my current age of fifty-six years that I came to realize what I really wanted to be in life – a Grand Pop! My daughter and son-in-law gave me that honor six months ago. Had I known how great it is to be Grand Pop – I would have skipped right over having children and gone right to Grand Pop. When I am with that little girl, there is nothing else in the world that matters. When I am not with her, I love politics and writing.

FOLLOW **FAIRWAY FRANK**

Fairway Frank has a blog where he shares his thoughts and observations on a frequent basis. As world events unfold, new issues will arise. Learn what Fairway Frank is thinking about at:

www.fairwayfrank.com

You can join in on the discussion by leaving your comments on this blog too. The blog will be active through the Election 2012 campaign season.

Now, go talk politics to your friends and family. Remember to conduct those discussions with an open mind – and keep the discussion civil. Now that you have read the book, you are a foot soldier in Fairway Frank's army. Together, we will reclaim civility in American politics by demonstrating the statesmanship that we want from our elected representatives!

www.ingramcontent.com/pod-product-compliance
Lightning Source LLC
Chambersburg PA
CBHW030349290526
45785CB00004B/1671